Collecting
Militaria

Collecting
Militaria

R. J. Wilkinson-Latham

John Gifford
London : 1975

First published in Great Britain 1975
John Gifford Ltd
125 Charing Cross Road
London, WC2H 0EB

TO CHRISTINE AND EDWARD

ISBN 0 7171 0483 1

Colour Plates by Hope Printers Ltd, London and Abingdon

Text printed Offset Litho in Great Britain by
Cox & Wyman Ltd
London, Fakenham and Reading

Contents

List of Plates (Colour)

List of Plates (Black and White)

77. Danish: Contemporary drawings of grenadier cap and coat 1789
78. Danish: Officer of the Royal Horse Guard *circa* 1804
79. Danish: Musketeer of 2nd Jutland Regiment 1828
80. Danish: Infantryman 1842
81. Danish: Dragoons 1858
82. Danish: The *Gardehussarregiment* on winter manœuvres wearing the pelisse 1886
83. Danish: Infantryman 1910
84. Austro–Hungarian: Line infantry 1800
85. Austro–Hungarian: Line infantry 1830
86. Austro–Hungarian: Hussars 1850
87. Austro–Hungarian: Line infantry 1900
88. Austro–Hungarian: Dragoons 1914. Left to right: sergeant-major, corporal, trooper
89. American: Officer's coat, New York Militia *circa* 1777
90. American: Brigadier-General's uniform *circa* 1809 with lapels buttoned back and coat hooked
91. American: General Staff Officer's coatee 1821–31
92. American: Dragoon Sergeant, winter dress 1833–50
93. American: Dress uniforms, Union infantrymen *circa* 1864
94. American: Fatigue uniform, Civil War period 1865
95. American: Sergeant, Light Artillery 1864–71
96. American: Infantryman, 5th New York Volunteers Infantry (Zouaves). One of the number of regiments on both sides during the Civil War which adopted Zouave-style uniforms
97. American: Captain's coat, Confederate State Artillery *circa* 1865
98. British: Houshold Cavalry breastplate and back-plate, *circa* 1820
99. Belgian: Cuirassiers' helmet and breastplate and back-plate *circa* 1850
100. French: Cuirassiers' helmet and breastplate and back-plates *circa* 1845
101. Russian: Officer's helmet and cuirass, Life Guard Horse Guard *circa* 1860
102. British: Sabretache, 16th Light Dragoons *circa* 1799
103. British: Sabretache, 5th Dragoon Guards *circa* 1815
104. British: Sabretache, 11th Hussars *circa* 1865
105. British: Undress pouch and sabretache, Westmorland and Cumberland Yeomanry *circa* 1880
106. French: Sabretache, Republican 9th Regiment of Cavalry *circa* 1790
107. Russian: Sabretache, Life Guard Hussar Regiment 1855–81
108. British: Epaulette, Commissariat Staff Corps officer *circa* 1816
109. Austrian/Bavarian: Austrian pouch, Austrian pouch, Bavarian pouch and belt
110. British: Rear view of a hussar trooper's equipment *circa* 1855 (reproduction)
111. British: Infantry pattern equipment *circa* 1850 consisting of knapsack, mess tin in oilskin cover, cross-belt for bayonet, cross-belt for pouch and water canteen
112. American: Infantry equipment *circa* 1850 consisting of waistbelt with clasp, small pouch for percussion caps, cross-belt and large pouch
113. British: Officer's shabraque, 3rd Dragoon Guards 1847
114. German: Various patterns of shabraques and horse furniture *circa* 1890
115. British: Selection of cavalry-sergeant's arm badges, regular and yeomanry
116. British: Cross-belt plates. Top row left to right: 83rd Foot 1840–50, Coldstream Guards *circa* 1831, Royal Artillery 1833–48. Centre row left to right: 31st Foot (*Note:* numbers on plate have been reversed after cleaning in error), 49th Foot 1843–55, 74th Foot *circa* 1875. Bottom row left to right: Royal Marine Light Infantry *circa* 1850, 28th Foot *circa* 1850, 7th Foot Light Company *circa* 1812

117. British: Helmet plate, collar badge and waistbelt clasp, 1st Berwick Rifle Volunteer Corps *circa* 1880. From original pattern drawing
118. British: Gorgets, shako plates and beltplates: Gorget, Dunfermline Volunteers *circa* 1810; shako plate, East Middlesex Militia *circa* 1850; Gorget *circa* 1800; waistbelt clasp, heavy cavalry *circa* 1815; cross-belt plate, Honourable East India Company *circa* 1800; cross-belt plate, King's Own Borderers *circa* 1860; helmet plate, 1st Volunteer Battalion Middlesex Regiment *circa* 1905; cross-belt plate, 57th Foot *circa* 1850
119. British: Pattern book drawing of 92nd purse or sporran *circa* 1848
120. British: Recruiting poster for Royal Lancashire Volunteers
121. Post cards including British, French and German. Note the various illustrated ones and the First World War prisoner and troop correspondence cards
122. Curios: 'Gentleman in khaki' 1900; ashtray in the form of a peaked cap made from an 18 pdr shell case; German prisoner-of-war medallion made in the Isle of Man; 'Gentleman in khaki' medallion 1900
123. Curios: Princess Mary's Gift Fund cigarette box and bullet pencil, Christmas 1914
124. British: Drum-Major's sash, 5th Northumberland Fusiliers
125. Swedish: Side drum *circa* 1700
126. British: Side drum, 42nd Highlanders *circa* 1820
127. British: Coldstream Guards colour *circa* 1820
128. British: 11th Light Dragoon's guidon *circa* 1780
129. Russian: Regimental colour, Seminov Life Guard Regiment 1700
130. Swedish: Artillery colour 1716

Introduction

The word 'Militaria', not to be found in the dictionary, is used to describe in global terms all items of uniform, head-dress and equipment, badges, drums, colours, buttons belonging to an officer or soldier. Sometimes it is extended to firearms, but usually swords, small arms and bayonets are treated as separate items. There are some collectors who do not hold with the use of the word 'Militaria' and I apologise to them in advance for its use, but until another better word is found to describe the collecting of military items of a wide and varied nature, the word 'Militaria' is, I feel, both descriptive and yet loose enough to include any item that has the slightest military connection.

Acknowledgements

It would have been impossible to compile a book on the wide aspects of Militaria which covers numerous countries and periods without the help of museums and collectors, who all gave freely of their time and knowledge towards this book. I would particularly like to thank the following for the time, trouble and energy they expended on my behalf and for answering numerous queries or helping with the illustrations: Boris Mollo, of the National Army Museum; John Mollo; Roy Butler of Wallis and Wallis; Captain R. G. Hollies-Smith, The Parker Gallery; J. R. Leconte, Musée Royal de L'Armée, Brussels; Inga Fl. Rasmussen, Tøjhusmuseet, Copenhagen; W. Hofrat, Heeresgeschtliches Museum, Vienna; and Karin Oscarsson, Kungl Armemuseum, Stockholm.

The illustrations have been selected from numerous sources to show actual items of Militaria as well as how, where and when they were worn. A selection of items comes from museums and others from auction houses and dealers to illustrate the types of fine items still to be found.

The colour photographs, except those from the Musée de L'Armée, Paris, were taken by my brother and to him my thanks. I must also thank my mother and father for allowing me to disrupt their collection of militaria to select items for photography.

Not every aspect of Militaria can be covered in a book of this nature but it is hoped that the pages which follow will give the reader an insight, introduction and appetite for the vast field of collecting Militaria.

R. J. WILKINSON-LATHAM

1 : Uniforms

By the early 1700s most of the European armies were dressed with some degree of uniformity within each arm of the service. From the mixture of colours that had been used during the seventeenth century, certain predominant colours emerged in military uniforms and these were still used by most armies, except for their bodyguard troops, until the general demise of full dress in 1914. In Britain, red had established itself as the predominant colour for coats in both infantry and cavalry, while Catholic countries tended towards white or light grey. In France royal troops adopted blue while the general infantry preferred white. In Russia the infantry showed a marked preference for dark green while in Sweden blue, with yellow cuffs, was adopted during the first decade of the eighteenth century. Prussia, who had issued strict clothing regulations as early as 1685, adopted dark blue, a colour that was to predominate Prussian and later Imperial German uniforms until the adoption in the first years of the twentieth century of field grey.

However, the introduction of what were later to be considered national colours of uniforms—the British 'red coat', the French blue, the Prussian blue and the Russian green—took decades to implement and become widespread. The Royal Scottish Regiment of Dragoons, later the Royal Scots Greys, were dressed in grey coats in 1683 and General Dalzell 'finding that he cannot be provided in this kingdom with as much cloth of one colour as will be clothes to the regiment . . .' asked permission from the Privy Council of Scotland to import '2,536 ells of stone-grey cloth' from England. However, by 1688 an account of money given to the quarter-master for the 'Expense of their coats' details:

5½ ells red cloth 2s. Scots pr. ell	£11:00:00
6 ells blew serge for lyneing at 1s. pr. ell	£06:00:00
Half ell green canvass for bindings	£00:04:00
10 dozen tin buttons at 5s. pr. doz	£02:10:00

There was, at this period, nothing basically 'military' about the dress of the soldier except the uniformity of colour, a necessary step taken for economic measures when bulk purchasing of cloth of one particular shade greatly reduced the cost of clothing the soldier. The coats worn by soldiers were almost identical to the style in vogue for civilians:

single-breasted, long skirts, closed collar, wide deep cuffs and pocket flaps on the back hip. A good example of a typical infantryman of the mid-eighteenth century, shown in Plate 70, is a private of the Söder-manland Regiment wearing the uniform prescribed in 1756. Some armies it seemed could not decide on the colour they preferred and the Saxon infantry, having adopted red, changed to white in 1734 while other countries keeping the basic colours preferred to change either the colour of the collar and cuffs or the lining.

The main departure from civilian styles lay in the head-dress and accoutrements of the soldier and in the wearing of gaiters or spatter-dashes which first came into use in the latter years of the seventeenth century. When armies had to march across difficult or muddy terrain carrying, or wearing, their entire clothing and often days of rations without supply trains or commissariat, it was necessary that what a soldier wore lasted. Most armies dressed their infantry in breeches with woollen stockings and black shoes but under harsh conditions the stockings would either get wet or torn. The spatterdashes, either in black or white canvas, adequately protected the legs to mid-thigh level and buttoned on the outside of the leg and were fitted with a strap passing under the shoe.

Once the initial problem of adopting a certain coloured uniform to distinguish one army from another had been solved, regimental differences were needed to further distinguish the wearer. The collar and cuffs were the obvious place for such features and when the fashion was to wear the coat open with lapels visible the different colours were extended to cover these. The placing of buttons on the coat, either singly or in pairs or other combinations, also served as a special regimental feature as did the later fashion of binding the button-holes and edging the coat in white or coloured lace. Although first used as a prudent economy measure against wear and tear, coloured tape soon, in Britain at least, developed into a complicated system of coloured lines or designs to pick out one regiment from another. In some armies regiments found that they were wearing the same coloured facings (as they became known) as another and so without infringing any clothing regulations that might have laid down a certain colour for the regiment they con-veniently changed the tone of the facing colour. There are many instances of this in the British army where a vast number of shades of green were worn: gosling green, willow green, grass green, etc.

The cavalry of most armies also wore the simple coat with deep cuffs of the infantry but did not necessarily follow the colour chosen by the infantry. For comfort when mounted cavalry took to buttoning back the coat skirts; a habit also adopted by the infantry when marching, to keep the legs free. Even at the beginning of the seventeenth century armour was still much in evidence although by now reduced to a breast- and back-plate and more often than not, in an attempt to reduce the weight of the mounted man, to just a breastplate.

Another basic item of uniform was the waistcoat which was worn by both infantry and cavalry under the top coat. In some armies the waistcoat matched the colour of the top coat while in others it was in the colour of the collar and cuffs, i.e. the facings. Some individual regiments departed completely from the above and had waistcoats that matched their breeches, as in Prussia where the breeches and waistcoats were either white, pale yellow or straw coloured.

The war of the Spanish Succession was the first time since the forma- tion of standing armies that Britain had been engaged on a large scale on the continent of Europe; during the rest of the eighteenth century the various European conflicts that brought together a number of nations as allies served as a 'market place' for new designs and ideas for military uniforms. The thought which induced many armies to emulate other designs, usually those of the victor in a war, was that a successful army was worthy of copying because perhaps in their organisation lay the secret of their success. It is not surprising, there- fore, to find a great similarity in cut and shape of uniforms in many countries throughout the seventeenth century and later. One of the most worthy of copying was the army of Frederick the Great of Prussia whose groundwork served the Prussian army well for nearly two hundred years, and whose 'New Regulations for the Prussian Infantry' was so well thought of that an English translation was published in London in 1757. To show the extent to which Frederick the Great went to make his soldiers the smartest and finest in Europe, the London edition of the 'New Regulations' stated the following concerning dress:

One of the essential parts of the *Prussian* service is that Regularity which is so carefully attended to from the highest Officer down to the private Man; the Soldier being obliged to hold himself in con- tinual Readiness to parade, is by that means kept constantly employed in preserving his Arms, Clothes, Accoutrements and Person in proper Order . . .

All Soldiers and non-commissioned Officers, are to put on their Gaiters before they are dressed; and that there may be no wrinkles in them, a false Calf is fixed, so as to fill up the Hollow between the inside of the Knee and the Calf of the leg.

When a Soldier is to appear on parade, or to Mount Guard, the Buttons of his Gaiters and every thing of Brass about him must be perfectly bright. Every year in the month of *May* the whole Army is new clothed from Head to Foot, and the old Clothes the Soldiers 15 are allowed to sell, the Facings and Collars being first cut off . . .

In the British army such rigidity was not so insisted on but fastidious colonels could award some startling punishments for slight errors in dress, such as the occasion when a private of the 10th Foot was awarded 100 lashes with the cat-o'-nine-tails for allowing the queue of his hair to fall off when on duty. Clothing in the British army was provided by the Colonel who under the propriety system 'owned' the regiment, supplied the clothing and equipment and emblazoned his own coat-of-arms on the colours and other appointments. The design of the clothing was purely a matter of personal choice although for economical reasons those of the other ranks in the army were similar in shape and cut, the officers only allowing themselves the latitude of extra embroidery and finery if they wished. Money was deducted from the men's pay to provide their food and lodging and another part known as the 'net off reckonings' paid for, or at least contributed towards the cost of, clothing and arms. The system was wide open to fraud which constantly occurred, the Paymaster-General in 1702 being forced to resign over the misappropriation of public money.

In 1703 the Office of the Controller of Army Pay Accounts was created with, among its duties, the inspecting of all clothing obtained under contract and ensuring that the cost did not exceed the 'off-reckonings'. In 1704 a Board of General Officers was created which controlled the contracting of clothing, each firm submitting samples which were checked with the sealed pattern before the contract was approved. The Board laid down the following concerning the clothing of the soldier:

> 1st year a good full bod'd cloth coat well lined which may serve for a waistcoat the 2nd year, a waistcoat, pair of good kersey breeches, pair of good stockings, pair of good shoes, 2 neck cloths, good strong hat well laced.
>
> 2nd year: a good strong coat lined as first year, waistcoat made of former years coat, pr strong new kersey breeches, pr good strong stockings, pr of strong shoes, a good shirt and neck cloth and a good strong hat well laced.

Britain

(a) INFANTRY

The most important pictorial evidence concerning the uniforms worn by the British infantry in the middle of the eighteenth century are the various coloured plates executed at the command of the Duke of

Cumberland and entitled *A Representation of the Cloathing of His Majesty's Household, and of all the Forces upon the Establishment of Great Britain and Ireland, 1742*. The book shows some 102 plates depicting the cavalry, foot guards and infantry of the line, marines, and a few untitled plates that are thought to be independent companies.

Each plate clearly shows the cut of the coat which was wide with full, long skirts turned back and buttoned revealing the lining. In most cases the coat was double-breasted with the lapels buttoned back to show the lining. Certain regiments did not have lapels and contented themselves with buttons and button-loops in lace, these being the 18th, 20th, 32nd, 38th and one of the independent companies. In most cases the lining matched the facing colour of the lapels and cuffs which were originally only an extension of the lining; but certain regiments, namely the 24th and 33rd, are depicted with white facings to the turnbacks even though their cuffs and lapels are green and red respectively.

The lapels and cuffs in the facing colour were ornamented with button-loops of regimental pattern tape set in a variety of patterns. The shape of the deep, wide cuff also varied, some having a dip in the centre with the top edge piped in lace while others had a round cuff with three or more tape button-loops and buttons.

The waistcoats are in nearly every case red, the same as the top coat, and edged down the front and around the bottom with regimental pattern lace but some regiments have waistcoats of the facing colour, namely the 30th, 35th, 39th and 43rd. Red breeches were the usual lower garment worn together with white or black gaiters or spatter-dashes that reached to above the knee. In some regiments blue breeches were preferred, especially so by the three regiments of foot guards. Other regiments wearing blue were the 7th, 9th and 21st.

In 1751 a Royal warrant, issued to regulate the dress and accoutrements of the army, described only the facing colours of the infantry and not their uniform although colours, drums, drummers' clothing and grenadier caps are all described. Presumably it was thought that the sealed pattern system set up under Marlborough would suffice in determining the uniform, although it was thought necessary to describe the uniform of the cavalry in the same warrant. Luckily for the student of military uniforms, David Morier executed a large number of paintings of privates and grenadiers of the line in 1751 which gives ample information on the clothing worn at the time.

The first noticeable difference between the 1742 book and Morier's 1751 paintings is in the shape of the lapels which button higher on the coat and are straight on the outer edge rather than curving in towards the waist. The coat was much larger and looser than previously and many regiments had, according to Morier's paintings, changed the

17

design of their distinctive regimental pattern lace. When the coat was worn buttoned over, the waist belt was worn over the top but when the lapels were buttoned back showing the facing colour, the belt was worn under the coat but over the waistcoat. The 24th and 33rd still retained their white lining to the turnbacks.

In 1768 a new warrant was issued which this time described the coats in full and noted that each regiment was to have its number on their buttons, although this had been ordered in 1767. The warrant goes to great lengths concerning all items of dress of privates and grenadiers up to officers. The 'private Men's Coats' were to be:

> . . . looped with Worsted Lace, but no Border. The Ground of the Lace to be White with Coloured Stripes. To have White Buttons. The Breadth of the Lace which is to make the Loop around the Button-Hole, to be about Half an Inch. Four Loops to be on the Sleeves, and four on the Pockets, with two each Side of the Slit behind.

The lapels, sleeves and pockets were strictly regulated as to size and position:

> The Breadth of all the Lapels to be three Inches to reach down to the Waist, and not to be wider at Top than at the Bottom. The Sleeves of the Coats to have a small Round Cuff, without any Slit, and to be made so that they may be unbuttoned and let down. The Whole to have Cross Pockets but no Flaps to those of the Waitcoat . . .

Plate 33 shows an other rank's coat of the 1st Foot Guards *circa* 1772. Both officers and men were ordered black gaiters with black buttons, and small stiff tops with black garters and buckles.

The previous use of the old coat to provide a waistcoat was stopped and waistcoats were plain, reaching now to just below the waist instead of above the knees, and white to match the linings and turnbacks of the coat. Light companies, however, retained the red waistcoat. A good general idea of the dress of the fighting soldier of *circa* 1790 is the water-colour of a private of the Coldstream Guards by Edward Dayes (Plate 34).

The experiences of the troops engaged in North America during the Revolutionary War showed that the long-tailed coat was anything but practical in heavily wooded country. Light infantry already cut their coats down to a minimum for comfort and ease of movement but after peace was declared in 1783 the lesson learned seemed to have been forgotten and once more the uniform returned to its former shape.

In 1789 the French Revolution exploded and for the next twenty-seven years an almost continuous state of war would exist in Europe, involving nearly every country in the conflict. It was during this war that once again styles and fashions of opposing or allied armies began to be noticed and copied. In 1796 the former long coat, which fastened at the upper chest and had the lapels buttoned back and sloped away to reveal the waistcoat, was replaced with a short-tailed coat which fastened down the front with a single row of buttons and was decorated with bands of tape across the chest. For officers this was double-breasted and lined in the facing colour so that it could be worn closed, with the top two buttons undone and turned back to reveal small triangles of facing, or buttoned back completely like the old coat and the front joined with hooks and eyes. On each shoulder was worn an epaulette in worsted: a small tuft for centre companies and a half-moon shaped 'wing' for flank companies, the light and grenadier.

The white breeches and black gaiters were still worn but white overalls, which were in reality the breeches and gaiters in one, were worn on active service; these were replaced in 1812 by blue-grey overalls or trousers with which were worn short gaiters in black or grey.

After the battle of Waterloo and the return, at last, of peace to Europe, 'important' matters such as uniforms and dress could again be considered. The extravagant styles of the Regency period coupled with the styles of the allies noted during the occupation of Paris resulted in the uniform becoming tighter and more ornate, although that of the rank and file did not alter to any extent, the red coat still being ornamented with the loops of regimental pattern tape and adorned with the various types of worsted tufted epaulettes.

When the Regent became George IV in 1820 he did much to further the elegance of the military uniform. Dress Regulations for the Army, describing officers' uniforms, were first issued in 1822 and they dictated exactly what would be worn and on what occasion, but as with all regulations they were not always strictly adhered to, especially among the cavalry where numerous regimental variations abounded.

In 1830 William IV ascended the throne and immediately set about reducing the embroidery and therefore the cost of uniforms. He was not, however, adverse to some dabbling with designs himself. In 1832 breeches for rank and file were finally abolished and the following year a red welt was added to the 'Oxford mixture' trousers. The biggest upheaval, which must have had the reverse effect on the King's economy measures, was the abolition in 1830 of silver lace in regular regiments, all of which were now ordered to wear gold lace and gilt buttons.

In 1835 ball tufts were placed on the shakos instead of hair plumes and the following year the various complicated patterns of regimental pattern tape for other ranks were abolished; in their place plain tape, which had been previously worn by sergeants, was introduced. Sergeants were ordered a new double-breasted coat devoid of any adornment on the chest.

From the beginning of the reign of Queen Victoria until the Crimean War there were a few minor changes to the uniform. Sergeants' sashes lost their central stripe in the facing colour in 1845 and the false pocket flaps on the tails of officers' coats were removed in 1848. A typical idea of an infantryman's uniform of the Crimean period is shown in Plate 39, a photograph taken in the Crimea by Roger Fenton and showing a battalion company man of the 28th Foot. Plate 40 shows that the uniforms of the Highlanders had changed little since Waterloo.

Contact with the French in the Crimea, this time as allies, produced some drastic changes in the uniforms of the army. The French were seen to be more organised than the British, with better camp arrangements, commissariat and dress and, following the long-established rule, Britain copied from her new allies. In 1855 a radical change occurred: the tailed coat was swept away and in its place a tunic, double-breasted at first but in 1856 made single-breasted, was issued. Rather than the tightness that had previously governed the coat, looseness and comfort became the yardstick for the new tunic. Towards the end of the century the cut became less voluminous and various modifications were made concerning the shape of the cuffs—the flapped style being replaced in 1868 with a pointed cuff—and ranking, which until 1880 was placed on the collar, as the epaulettes on which it had previously been placed had disappeared in 1855.

Until well into the 1870s, red and later scarlet coats were the usual dress for parade wear and fighting but after the Indian mutiny khaki clothing started to make its presence felt. Basically only used in India in the 1860s and 1870s, it did not make its appearance in the British army until the last decade of the nineteenth century and then only for 'Foreign Service' and consequently adapted for hotter climates than Europe. After the Boer War a long, hard look was taken at British uniforms and a certain number of economy measures were made, articles of a superfluous nature being abolished. The lacing and embroidery on the officers' coats became simpler and therefore less expensive and a number of the former facing colours which had been abolished in 1881 under the new territorial regiment system in favour of four colours only—blue for Royal regiments, white for English and Welsh, yellow for Scottish and green for Irish—started to return.

In 1904 khaki uniforms were issued as a service dress and not confined to 'Foreign Service' only. With them a new set of equipment was introduced and scarlet was relegated solely to the parade ground and ceremonials. Khaki was also now used as the everyday working dress of the soldier and the era of individuality was slowly ending. In 1914 scarlet tunics were handed in and the army took the field in France in khaki which was from then on to be the uniform of the soldier. Between the wars officers were permitted to wear full dress on certain occasions, but it was not insisted upon.

(b) CAVALRY

The cavalry of the 1740s were dressed in a similar way to the infantry with their red coats, coloured lapels and laced button-loops but in 1751, the clothing warrant issued in that year describes the coat of a heavy dragoon as:

> ... lapelled to the waist with the colour of the regiment and lined with the same colour; Slit sleeves turned up with the colour of the lapel.

The coat for the Horse was:

> ... lapelled to the bottom with the colour of the regiment and lined with the same colour (except the fourth regiment of Horse, whose facings are black, and the lining Buff colour), small square Cuffs of the Colour of the lapel.

Dragoons' coats were to be without lapels and double-breasted with slit sleeves. Like the infantry, the waistcoat was now to be white or buff coloured. Rank distinction was by means of epaulettes; sergeants of dragoon guards, dragoons and light dragoons had epaulettes in the facing colour fringed in either gold or silver depending on the colour of the officers' regimental lace. Corporals had their epaulettes edged in yellow or white tape (there were no regimental pattern tapes with coloured lines etc in the cavalry) and fringed in silk. Dragoons were ordered to wear only one epaulette on the left shoulder but light dragoons wore two epaulettes. Regiments of horse, which now had almost disappeared, wore red shoulder straps.

In 1787 the appearance of the cavalryman was somewhat changed when it was ordered that the sword belt should be worn over the coat and that the pouch belt should be made narrower to match the sword belt. Dragoon guards were ordered epaulettes in the following year as a means of keeping the belts in place. In the same year the last regiments of horse were converted to dragoon guards, all taking white buttons and silver lace except the 7th Dragoon Guards who adopted gilt or brass buttons and gold lace.

In 1796 the heavy cavalry were issued with a modified coat in which the skirts were made shorter and the pocket flaps dispensed with. Epaulettes were discontinued and shoulder straps with red wings fringed with white were added. The coat was single-breasted with the turnbacks faced in the colour of the collar and cuffs, bars of tape or lace on the chest and four buttons and false button-loops on each cuff.

In 1812 the heavy cavalry (the dragoon guards), altered their uniform to the appearance they were to retain to the end of the Napoleonic War and the Waterloo campaign. The coat was superseded by a new pattern which dispensed with the looping on the chest and cuffs, and introduced in its place a broad band of lace that went around the collar, down the front each side of the joining and around the skirts. Buttons were dispensed with and the coat was fastened with hooks and eyes. The cuffs also were ornamented with a broad band of lace. In 1819 the short coat was replaced by a coatee, with longer tails to the skirts and a return to buttons and bars of lace on the chest. Dragoon guards had the buttons and lace loops arranged in pairs, dragoons having them singly; dragoon guards had four lace loops and buttons on the cuffs and skirts, dragoons had only three.

During the campaigning of the latter years of the Napoleonic War around 1812, grey overalls with a red stripe were worn in the field; although it appears that red was not the only colour, the Royal Scots Greys being noted with blue stripes.

In 1822 the colour of stripes on the grey overalls was ordered to be in the facing colour for the men but in 1827 this distinction was withdrawn and yellow or white ordered.

In looking at the uniforms of the cavalry described above, we must not forget the light dragoons. They too had worn the lapelled coat but in 1784 there was a complete change in their style and mode of dress. The 'Regulation for the Clothing of the Regiments of Light Dragoons' dated 1784 ordered that:

> The Clothing of a Private Light Dragoon to consist of a Jacket, Shell, Under-Waistcoat, and Leather Breeches.
>
> The Jacket and Shell to be of Blue Cloth, the Collars and Cuffs of the Royal Regiments to be Red, and those of the other Regiments to be the Colour of the Facings of the Regiment, looped upon the Breast, and edged with White Thread Cord, and to be lined with White; the 11th and 13th Regiments excepted, which are to be lined with Buff.

The breeches were to be in buckskin and the regulation added further that:

> The Make of the Dress, and Method of placing the Cord upon the Breast of the Jacket, to be exactly comformable to the Pattern approved of by His Majesty.

A typical light dragoon dressed according to the above regulations is shown in Plate 35.

By the early years of the nineteenth century light dragoons completely changed their appearance to a remarkable closeness to the French style, it being said in the Peninsula that the outline of horsemen of light dragoons on a hill were often mistaken for French. The new coat was still blue but had lost the frogging on the chest. The turnbacks, piping and collar together with the plastron-shaped front were in the facing colour. Around the waist the men wore a girdle in blue stripes alternated with stripes of the facing colour (those of the officers were crimson and gold). The nether wear was blue-grey overalls with stripes down the outside seam, the bottom bound in leather.

However, a number of light dragoon regiments were affected by a more important change of dress in 1805, that of conversion to the hussar pattern. The short jacket was heavily braided or frogged, as the term was, in cord and braid in the regimental colour (gold or silver, other ranks having yellow or white) and the collar and cuffs were in the facing colour of the regiment. A girdle or barrel sash was worn around the waist and white pantaloons and knee boots completed the uniform. Another item of true hussar dress was the pelisse which was a fur trimmed and lined 'overcoat' which could be worn when necessary or slung over the left shoulder in a rakish fashion. The copying of continental hussars extended beyond the bounds of dress, however, and long moustaches were soon in evidence.

Under campaign conditions, the white pantaloons soon gave way to overalls as being more practical but for full dress white and, later, blue pantaloons were worn.

In 1816 some remaining regiments of light dragoons were converted into lancers, retaining the light dragoon style of coat which was kept, with modifications, up until the Crimean War. Light dragoons also retained this style of coat with some modifications again up until the Crimean War.

Returning to the dragoons and dragoon guards in 1830, when William IV ascended the throne, we find that the loops of lace on the breast have disappeared and the style of coatee altered by having the collar entirely in the facing colour and of course the radical change to gilt buttons and gold lace. William IV's penchant for red altered completely the look of the light dragoons who were now ordered red coats and the abolition of the lapels on the front which formed the plastron shape. With the hussars a certain amount of opposition was met, and a compromise of having only the pelisses in red was arrived at. The lancers as well were not exempt and soon they were all wearing the red or scarlet coatee which was double-breasted and had lost the coloured lapels of the previous style of coatee.

The heavy cavalry remained virtually unchanged in their uniform   23 until 1847 when the skirts of the coatee were shortened and squared off.

In 1840 blue jackets were once again introduced for light dragoons, with blue pelisses for hussars and lancers, except for the 16th (Plate 3) who retained a scarlet coat up until the demise of full dress.

In 1855 the entire cavalry came under the same drastic changes that had affected the infantry. The coatees of the heavy cavalry, the light dragoon and lancers were abolished. The short jacket of the hussars was also done away with although the Royal Horse Artillery managed to keep a simplified version which they wore up until the end of full dress, and which is still worn today on ceremonial occasions by King's Troop R.H.A.

The simplified uniforms of the cavalry were very much in line with that designed for the infantry. The dragoons and dragoon guards, following the Prussian lead given some fifteen years before, adopted a tunic which was single-breasted with collar and cuffs showing the facing and individuality of the regiment. Light dragoons wore a blue coat and lingered on in the British army until 1861 when the remaining regiments were converted to hussars. Lancers adapted their double-breasted coats into tunics which were buttoned over but allowed to be buttoned back revealing a 'butterfly' lapel. Later, the tunic was made either to button across to show all blue (the 16th excepted, who showed all red) or to button the opposite way, revealing the plastron in the facing colour. Hussars also adopted the jacket but managed to retain an elementary form of frogging; this time a simple affair of bars with loops and drops on the chest, and piping and Austrian knots on the back seams.

In essence these remained the tunics worn by the cavalry in full dress until 1914, although blue and red 'frock' tunics were introduced for service wear later in the century and khaki, as it had done in the infantry, soon appeared in the cavalry. In common with the infantry a khaki service dress was introduced in 1904 which with minor modifications was to be the uniform when the cavalry of the British Expeditionary Force took the field in France in 1914.

As with other arms of the service full dress was permitted for officers between the wars, and also for bands as a useful recruiting aid but the assassination of Archduke Ferdinand at Sarajevo ended an era of over 200 years of full dress in the armies of Europe.

France

(a) INFANTRY

As with head-dress, the political change brought about by the French Revolution did not alter uniforms to any great extent. In October 1789 regulations were issued to govern the style of uniforms and the infantry were ordered to wear, as they had done previously, white coats with collar, cuffs and lapels of a distinctive regimental colour. The style of uniform was similar to that worn in the British army: a long-tailed coat with skirts turned back, lapels buttoned back and the coat hooked up at the chest to reveal a white waistcoat. White breeches and black gaiters were the nether garments, white gaiters being reserved for full dress wear. The first radical change occurred in 1793 when numbered regiments were abolished and a new system of demi-brigades established. Rather than continue with the white coat, the army was issued with a blue uniform which had been the style worn by the National Guard but this new measure took time to implement. The cut and style of the coat was similar to the previous white one and the infantry were ordered white lapels with red collar and cuffs and white piping. The nether wear was still the same.

Light infantry wore blue breeches with their blue coats, piped white and lapelled and cuffed in scarlet. *Voltigeurs* of line regiments and light infantry had yellow collar and cuffs which on occasion were probably buff coloured. In 1806 a move was made to re-introduce white uniforms but after a year, when few regiments had been re-uniformed in this way, the idea was dropped.

1812 was a most important year for the uniforms of the French and the infantry in particular. Lagging behind the other European countries by still clinging to the long coat, it was at last decided to introduce a more modern style of jacket. Because of shortages in supply and the complexities of re-equipping the large army that France possessed at this time, first battalions were singled out to receive the new clothing. The new jacket or *habit-veste* had short tails and fastened completely down the front with hooks and eyes yet still retained false buttons and lapels which were coloured white, the same as the collar. Epaulettes were dispensed with and shoulder straps introduced, the difference between *Grenadiers* or *Voltigeurs* being by means of red or yellow piping respectively.

After the defeat of Napoleon at Waterloo and his final exile, numbered infantry regiments were abolished and legions created in various French departments. Being Royalist troops a return was made to the traditional white uniform cut on similar lines to the *habit-veste* of 1812, each having a distinctive colour of collar, cuff and lapel. Distinctions between *Grenadiers*, *Voltigeurs*, etc were, on the jacket, by means of various devices on the turnbacks: a grenade for *Grenadiers*, for *Fusiliers* a fleur de lis and for *Voltigeurs* a French hunting horn. Blue uniforms were reserved for Royal troops only, as they had been previously.

In 1820 another major re-organisation of the French army affected the uniforms with white finally disappearing and blue becoming the predominant colour. Trousers at last made an appearance in place of breeches and gaiters and these were white for summer, a common practice in most armies at this time, and blue for winter. A new single-breasted blue coat was introduced with shorter tails than before and with distinctive collar colours, cuff piping and turnbacks. The regimental colouring was organised on a different system than in Britain. Colours of regiments were organised in fours: 1–4 had white, 5–8 crimson, 9–12 yellow, 13–16 rose, 17–20 orange, 21–24 light blue, 25–28 buff and 29–32 green. From 33 to 60 the colours repeated themselves in the same groups of four.

In 1828 this complicated and hardly satisfactory system was abandoned and all line regiments adopted scarlet, yellow being reserved for the light infantry. The following year a most important and permanent change occurred in the uniform of the French infantry. The blue trousers were replaced by red trousers, a feature which was to outlast all other uniform changes and nether wear in which the French infantry were to take the field in 1914.

Another important innovation which was to remain with the French army until 1914, and even 1940, was the wearing of the greatcoat with the skirts buttoned back reminiscent of the eighteenth-century uniforms. The greatcoat, first issued in 1822, was worn in Algeria in the 1830s and from then on seemed to be unofficially adopted in place of the tunic for fighting or service dress.

In 1845 a further complete change was made in the uniform of the infantry. Following the Prussian lead, the coatee was discarded and the tunic introduced. It was rather longer and fuller below the waist than the Prussian version and piped and faced as previously. The greatcoat, which was now tending towards blue rather than the authorised grey, continued to be worn in service dress and marching order and from contemporary prints appears to be hardly any longer than the three-quarter-length tunic.

By the time of the Crimean War the light infantry had been abolished and all infantry were faced in red. The greatcoat was now universally accepted as the fighting dress and straps were fitted to secure the epaulettes. The single-breasted tunic also had become slightly shorter but was still cut full in the skirts and later in 1855 served as the model for the British double- and later single-breasted tunic.

In 1860 a short, blue, single-breasted jacket was introduced with a yellow collar and a flap on the cuff. It was extremely short and waisted in an exaggerated fashion. With it, baggy red 'Zouave' type trousers were worn which ended mid-calf tucked into fawn leather leggings.

Over the lower part of the leggings and boot were worn white gaiters or spats. *Chasseurs à pied* did not wear the red trousers, preferring instead a darkish green with yellow welt on the outer seam of the leg. The *Chasseurs* also had an inverted, yellow, lace chevron on the cuff rather than the slashed flap and were further singled out by having white metal buttons.

In 1868 a double-breasted tunic was introduced which had a double row of seven buttons, and the baggy red trousers were replaced by ordinary red trousers for the infantry. The greatcoat continued to be worn as the usual fighting dress and the tunic only made its appearance on full dress ceremonial parades.

After the upheaval of the Franco–Prussian War and the fall of the Empire of Napoleon III, the same uniform continued in use until 1899 when a single-breasted blue tunic was sanctioned with red collar and flaps to the cuff. The regimental number appeared in red on a blue patch on the collar of the tunic and the greatcoat, both of which had been worn without epaulettes since 1872 as these decorations had been reserved for full dress wear only. The typical uniform worn by the infantry from the turn of the century until the first years of the First World War is illustrated in Plate 60, a photograph of 1908 which shows soldiers dressed in varying military uniforms of different eras.

In 1914 the French in their blue and red took the field alongside the British, sensibly dressed in khaki, and soon found that their uniform was not suitable for modern warfare. Along with other countries France had been experimenting with a more camouflaged type of uniform during the first decade of the century but, unlike the Germans and British, had not succeeded in introducing a general service dress. At the end of 1914 the red trousers and blue greatcoat were superseded by a greatcoat, tunic and trousers in horizon-blue and leather leggings were replaced by puttees. The colonial troops and Zouaves were issued with khaki uniforms of the same style. In 1935 the French at last abandoned horizon-blue and opted for khaki uniforms in the style of 1914. These continued to be worn in 1939 and 1940 until the Free French in Britain were supplied with British and, later, American uniforms.

Napoleon's Imperial Guard Grenadiers wore the same pattern coat as the line regiments with scarlet collar, cuffs and turnbacks and with white lapels, but piped in scarlet while the Guard *Chasseurs à pied* wore a similar coat with white piping. The other regiments of the Guard, the *Tirailleurs-Grenadiers*, had blue lapels to the regulation coat with red collars and red pointed cuffs. By Waterloo, the Imperial Guard had almost given up the white breeches and black gaiters in favour of blue trousers but they did not wear the 1812 jacket adopted by the rest of the infantry.

27

Although for a brief period between 1814–15 a new Royal Guard was formed, it was not until 1822 that a new, permanent Royal Guard was established. Wearing the same uniform as the line they were distinguished by nine bars of white tape sewn on the chest of the single-breasted coat while the 7th and 8th regiments, who were Swiss, had similarly cut red coats with bars of lace. These are shown in Plate 52. In 1854 Napoleon III established his new empire and with it an Imperial Guard which adopted long-tailed coatees for the *Grenadiers* and *Voltigeurs*: the former with white lapels forming a plastron and red collar and cuffs; the latter with yellow collar and turnbacks and pointed cuffs piped in yellow. The *Chasseurs à pied* of the Guard conformed to the usual infantry pattern uniform but it appears they had adopted the shorter-styled jacket before it became general wear in 1860.

In 1860 the Imperial Guard who wore the long-tailed coat of another era modernised with the rest of the army but instead of adopting the short jacket took the 1845 three-quarter-length coat into wear with the chest embellished with nine bars of tape, white for *Grenadiers* and yellow for *Voltigeurs*. The standard practice of red collar and cuffs for *Grenadiers* and yellow collar and cuffs for *Voltigeurs* was adhered to. Red trousers were worn with a blue welt down the outer seam. After 1870 all Imperial Guard distinctions disappeared and the regiments placed in the line. The dismounted section of the Republican Guard today still wears blue coats and shakos.

(b) CAVALRY

As in other European armies, the dress of the heavy cavalry was purely an extension of that worn by the infantry. Blue coats with distinctive colours of lapels, cuffs and turnbacks distinguished each of the regiments of the Royalist army from its neighbour. In 1791 the uniform was still the same but the face colours were, in the French manner, grouped in four groups, each regiment within the group wearing either scarlet, yellow, crimson or pink. In 1803 the heavy cavalry was split and the first thirteen regiments became *Cuirassiers* while the remaining six changed to dragoons.

By 1804 there existed twelve regiments of *Cuirassiers* in the Imperial army wearing blue coats, white breeches and knee boots. The regimental colours were in the usual French manner of grouping regiments and giving each group a colour. In 1812 a short-tailed coat was issued but otherwise the general appearance remained unchanged. Dragoons in the French army had worn green uniforms since 1763 and continued to do so during the 1st Empire. The coat was green with collars, lapels, cuffs and turnbacks in the authorised facing colour. White waistcoats were worn so as to be visible beneath the coat which, as in other arms of the service, fastened at the top of the chest and sloped away. White breeches and knee boots were the nether wear. In 1812 the general 'modernising' by the issue of short-tailed coats affected the dragoons who received theirs in a new system of regimental colours of cuffs, etc. The regiments were grouped in sixes: 1–6 having scarlet, 7–12 crimson, 13–18 rose, 19–24 yellow and 25–30 *aurore* which in fact tended to be a light orange colour. Dragoons continued to wear the short-tailed coat after Napoleon's defeat and under Louis-Philippe their colours, owing to a great reduction in number of regiments, were regulated in fours: 1–4 having rose, 5–8 yellow and 9 and 10 crimson.

Carabiniers, who in 1809 had been given cuirasses, wore short, white jackets with sky-blue collars; the distinction between the 1st and 2nd regiments was by the cuff colour, red for the 1st and blue for the 2nd. In 1831 the white jacket was replaced by one of sky-blue which was worn until 1866 when they were incorporated into the new Imperial Guard and in 1871 amalgamated into the line.

The red trousers with which the infantry had been issued in 1829 also pervaded into the cavalry and the grey trousers with piping in the regiment's colour were soon replaced by red trousers for dismounted wear and booted red overalls for mounted duties. In 1854 these trousers became wide and rather baggy and the leather re-inforce was heightened to appear like a boot. Plate 58 of a *Chasseur* shows these hugely exaggerated trousers in wear.

By the Crimean War, dragoons numbered twelve regiments, again divided for identification purposes into three groups of four: 1–4 having white, 5–8 yellow and 8–12 red. In each group the first two regiments had colours as above but the latter two, in green, had the cuff instead in the facing colour, a feature not accorded to the first two regiments. In 1867 dragoons were ordered to wear a single-breasted blue uniform with all regiments having white collar and flaps on the cuff.

Cuirassiers also were ordered red-booted overalls and wore these until the early years of the twentieth century when they were replaced by breeches and knee boots.

The French light cavalry consisted of *Chasseurs à cheval* who wore a hussar-type uniform in green with white piping and embroidery. The twelve regiments were divided for recognition into groups of three: the first regiment wearing collar and cuffs in the colour, the second the cuffs only and the third the collar. By 1816 the hussar-styled jackets had been replaced by green jackets with large lapels similar to the British light dragoons but by the time of Louis-Philippe a green single-breasted jacket with red trousers had been ordered. In 1853 they were ordered a hussar pattern jacket in green, frogged with eighteen loops of

29

black lace and with three rows of white metal buttons. For full dress wear the officer's jacket was frogged in silver.

Lancers were also part of the French light cavalry but the line regiments converted to this role did not adopt lancer-styled uniforms until the 1830s when they were ordered blue short-tailed coats with yellow plastron for the first four regiments and red for the other four. Individuality within each group was by the usual complicated system of varying collar, cuffs and turnbacks. In 1870 lancers disappeared from the French cavalry.

The other form of light cavalry was the hussars which the Royalist French army had maintained from the middle of the eighteenth century but of which, under the First Empire, there remained only six regiments; each was dressed in Imperial-blue breeches, dolman and pelisse with yellow collar and piping to the dolman, yellow stripes and frogging to the trousers, dolman and pelisse. By the restoration and the re-organisation in 1822 red trousers were worn by all but one regiment and the dolman and pelisses were given individuality by being made in distinctive colour: 1st sky-blue, 2nd maroon, 3rd light grey, 4th red, 5th dark blue and 6th green. The collars were red in all regiments excepting the 4th who with their red ensemble wore blue collars. In 1862 pelisses were abandoned. Regiments were further distinguished by the colour of the cuffs which was also adopted as the colour for the baggy booted overalls. The 1st, 3rd, 5th, 6th and 7th had red while the 2nd, 4th and 8th had sky-blue but the 2nd wore red trousers with a double stripe to the outside seam. In 1867 it was decided to dispense with the heavily frogged dolman and introduce a sky-blue jacket with elementary frogging of six rows of white but only the 1st and 8th regiments received them before the outbreak of the Franco–Prussian War. After the war light cavalry were given a light-blue dolman with nine rows of frogging with red collars. A similar jacket in dark blue but with seven rows of frogging was introduced in 1884 for infantry officers who wore it until 1893. By this time the entire French army was wearing the distinctive red trousers or breeches.

The uniforms of the Imperial and Royal Guards cavalry were similar to that of the line cavalry they corresponded to, but one main departure made by Napoleon III was the creation of the *Cent Garde* who wore sky-blue tunics and handsome cuirasses on mounted duty and a *surveste* in buff cloth for dismounted duty. Being the most senior of all regiments in France they took as their facing colour Imperial purple which was worn in undress in the form of coloured trousers. In 1870 they disappeared into the line of the new army.

As with the infantry during the First World War, the highly colourful *Cuirassiers* and dragoons, whose only concession to modern warfare seemed to be to wear brownish covers on helmets and cuirasses, took the field and found their uniforms impracticable for fighting in such conditions. Gradually horizon-blue was introduced and a steel helmet. Only the *Garde Republicaine* today continue the tradition of the helmeted cavalry of 1914 with their steel helmets, blue coats trimmed with red, white breeches and knee boots.

Prussia, German States and German Empire

(a) INFANTRY

The typical mid-eighteenth century style of uniform established for the Prussian army by Frederick the Great varied little during his lifetime but in 1786 the lapels of the blue coat, which had only been a sewn-on addition rather than a practical aspect of the coat, were made so that they could be buttoned over in a double-breasted fashion. *Fusiliers*, now élite light infantry, wore green uniforms with regimental facings. The cut of the coat was looser than that under Frederick the Great whose passion for tightness and unwrinkled appearance grew into a mania. The coat of 1786 still followed the style that pervaded most armies: long tails with turnbacks, lapels, and a white waistcoat visible under the coat.

When Prussia renewed the fight against Napoleon after 1806, a completely new uniform was chosen modelled closely on that of Russia. Plate 64 shows a typical infantryman and Plate 63 an officer wearing the new uniform. The main colour was blue and the coat was double-breasted with short tails at the back. The collar was high and open at the front revealing the stock and neck cloth. The cuffs were round with slashed flap panels and tight trousers in grey for active service were tucked into black gaiters. For parade-wear tight, white trousers were worn. The system of facing colours distinguished the place of origin of the regiment; those from East Prussia had brick-red, West Prussia crimson, Pomerania white, Brandenburg bright red, and pink for Silesia which was later changed to yellow. In 1817, however, this system was abandoned and all Prussian infantry adopted bright red facings. The tight breeches and gaiters also gave way to grey trousers with a red welt on the outside seam.

The same uniform was worn throughout the 1820s and '30s until 1842 when there was a radical change in the uniforms of the Prussian army. The double-breasted, tailed coat during the twenty-odd years of peace had once more assumed the tightness that marked a long period of peace in an army. The new tunic was single-breasted with eight brass buttons down the front, and the leading edge piped in red. The collar lost some of its height and was partially open at the front with   31 rounded tops. The cuffs changed from a round pattern with button-loops to a round pattern with slashed flap and three buttons. Privates had plain collars but N.C.O.'s had a band of lace on the top edge and also around the cuff. The rear of the tunic was decorated with slashed flap panels with buttons. The grey trousers with red welt continued to be worn with white ones reserved for ceremonial and parade wear.

Somewhat unconcerned about the French influence on European uniforms, Prussia pursued her own course and the appearance from 1842 until the outbreak of the First World War altered little in basic principles, only being streamlined and modified slightly. Although a great number of countries followed the French lead in uniform design, Prussia was not without followers. In 1845 Sweden adopted for its infantry and cavalry single-breasted tunics in the Prussian style and leather helmets but by 1854 had reverted again to a more French style. Schleswig-Holstein was another to follow the Prussian lead, providing tunics and helmets in the Prussian style in 1844. In 1852 the Principality of Palma hastily abandoned Austrian-styled uniforms for the Prussian pattern with leather helmets and single-breasted tunics. By the 1850s there were few individualists left, and uniforms tended to be either on the Prussian pattern or the French style, perhaps Austria alone being one of the marked 'abstainers' in the military 'fashion race'.

Although Prussia held a sway over the other Germanic States in uniform matters because of their close political ties, the member States still maintained some measure of individuality in their uniforms, but each at some period up until the formation of the empire abandoned much of their individuality in adopting the Prussian pattern. Mecklenberg-Schwerin adopted the blue tunic with red collar, cuffs and piping in 1848 but with silver lace to distinguish N.C.O.'s while the Hanoverians, having switched from the British style in 1837 when William IV died, adopted the Prussian style and took to the tunic in 1849. The Bavarians wore their distinctive light-blue uniforms and adopted the tunic in 1848 on which they continued the regimental system of colours re-adopted in 1826. In 1873 the Bavarian regiments conformed more to the Prussian style but continued to use the light-blue colour with red collars and cuffs.

In Saxony regiments green tunics were replaced by blue in 1862 and collar, cuffs and piping coloured according to brigades but in 1867 when they became part of the North German Federation they adopted the Prussian dark-blue tunics. Wurttemberg adopted medium-blue tunics in 1849 which differed from the normal pattern made popular by the Prussians in being double-breasted with the regiments distinguished by varying colour collar patches. 1st wore white, 2nd black, 3rd orange, 4th green, 5th pale blue, 6th blue, 7th dark red and 8th yellow with the company number embroidered on the shoulder strap.

1. Sabretache, Royal Artillery circa *1850; Silver flap pouch, heavy cavalry* circa *1860; Leather helmet, Fife Mounted Rifles* circa *1870; Lt-Colonel's epaulette, William IV* circa *1835*

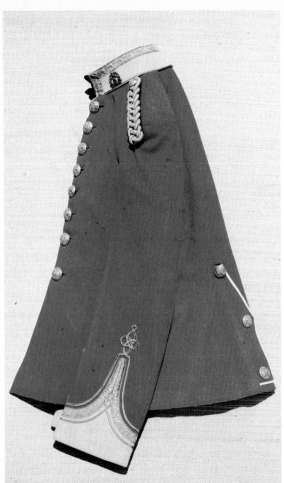

2. *Officer's tunic of the Middlesex
Regiment* circa 1904

3. *Other rank's tunic and lance cap
of the 16th Lancers* circa 1906

In 1871 they adopted a uniform more in line with the Prussian pattern but managed to keep the distinctive double-breasted feature until 1892.

When the German Empire was proclaimed in 1871, the various States that made up the new Imperial army had adopted the uniforms dictated by the leader, Prussia, although as described above a number kept individual distinctions. Although the Prussian style was prevalent, various details of State or regimental tradition were still allowed.

Like the British army, Germany had rifle troops and *jager* battalions which dressed in green with red collars, cuffs and shoulder straps to denote their role. However, green was not solely the colour of the riflemen; the Saxon field-artillery wore it as did the *Garde jager* and *Schutzen* battalions, the former with red collar and cuffs and the latter with black collar and cuffs with a slashed flap and three buttons.

Germany too had developed a 'Foreign Service' uniform before the turn of the century, made in grey cloth piped in white for East Africa and red for the Cameroons. Plate 66 shows a photograph of the Kaiser in the Foreign Service uniform. By 1901 various new designs of service dress had been considered and in 1907 were issued on a limited scale. In 1910 the whole army was issued with field-grey uniforms for field service and manœuvres. Unlike the British army where the service dress was of a universal pattern for all arms of the service, the German *Waffenrock* came in a variety of styles. In the infantry it was similar to the full dress tunic but with a stand-and-fall collar and two pockets below the waist. The tunic had no facings but was piped in scarlet down the front and around the cuff, collar, slashed flaps and the back. The slashed piped flaps on the cuff were later dispensed with on the *Bluse* introduced in 1915.

In the cavalry the field-grey uniforms followed the style of the full-dress uniforms.

(b) CAVALRY

Just as the re-organisation on Russian lines of the Prussian infantry radically changed uniform styles, so it did in the cavalry. The change can be seen in comparing Plate 61 showing an officer of the *Garde du Corps* of 1790 and Plate 62 which shows the uniform worn in 1809. The coat was double-breasted with a high, red collar open at the front showing the neck cloth with round, red cuffs decorated with button-loops and buttons. Each shoulder sported an epaulette with rounded end. The overalls were grey with a red welt and with a row of buttons down the outside seam of each leg. The rest of the cavalry was divided into *Cuirassiers*, hussars, *Uhlans* or lancers and dragoons.

Cuirassiers were dressed similarly to the *Garde du Corps* in white with various colours of cuffs and collars as well as silver or gold lace on the officers' uniforms depending on the regimental custom. In 1806, including the *Garde du Corps* there were thirteen regiments of *Cuirassiers* with individual colouring and facing which were altered in 1808 to conform to the following colours of collar and cuff: *Garde du Corps* red; Silesia black, East Prussia blue and Brandenburg red, and at the same time the colour of the buttons was rationalised along the same lines: white for the *Garde du Corps*, yellow for Silesia, white for East Prussia and yellow for Brandenburg.

In 1819 the button on the side of the grey-booted overalls was done away with and a return was made to regimental facing colours rather than grouping by areas. In 1843 the drastic changes in uniform involved the issue of tunics and a new helmet to the *Cuirassiers*, the tunic being white with collar, cuffs and two lines each side of the front opening in the facing colour. Cuffs and collars for officers were trimmed with lace. The same pattern of overalls, dark grey with a red welt, was retained. A special feature of the white *koller* as it was called was that the armholes, sleeves and back seams were piped in a special regimental colour. Plate 6 shows a contemporary print by Verlag and Druck and Saches and Co. of Berlin showing a *Cuirassier* of the 6th regiment with blue collar and piping to the white tunic. Cuirasses were not worn after 1888 for anything but parade wear. By 1865 tight, white breeches with 'Brandenburg' boots were being worn. This footwear came up to mid-thigh but by 1888 had been replaced in most regiments, except *Guard Cuirassier's*, by knee boots. A jacked boot was worn by *Guard Cuirassier* officers in full dress. While the white *koller* made an attractive display on parades it was considered anything but practical for warfare and a tunic in the same style but in dark blue was issued for service wear towards the end of the century. In 1910 the field-grey tunic and breeches for service wear were issued to *Cuirassiers* who were distinguished by the lines of piping around the top and front of the collar and cuffs and also by their jacked boots.

In the dragoon regiments, in 1808, the traditional cornflower-blue coats were worn; these were double-breasted with the collar and round cuffs in the regimental facing colour. The overalls, reinforced around the bottom of, and inside, each leg, were in grey with grey cloth-covered buttons which in 1812 were changed to match those on the coat. In 1815 the buttons were abolished and grey overalls with a red stripe on the outside seam issued. In 1808 the regimental colours had followed the favourite system in Prussia at that time of designating regiments by area, six colours being used in 1808–19, reduced to four in that year. The head-dress worn was similar to the infantry shako.

In 1843 cornflower-blue tunics were issued with a patch in the regimental colour on the front of the collar. The cuffs were round and, for the officers, edged in lace as was the collar. The back of the tunic had two slashed flap panels. Plate 6 shows an officer of the 2nd Dragoon Regiment with the black facing colour. Except for a slight tightening-up in style from the rather loose garment of 1843, there were only minor changes in dragoon dress. In 1910, in common with the rest of the Imperial army, the field-grey service dress was issued to dragoons. In 1915 the modified field *bluse* was issued to all cavalry and many of the minor dress distinctions were, for economy reasons, abolished.

Hussars followed the uniform styles adopted in all other countries that employed this type of cavalry with heavily frogged dolmans, frogged and fur-trimmed pelisses, and tight, leather-reinforced overalls. Unlike hussar regiments in the British army, where a basic uniform colour was adopted and then embellished with facing colours and gold or silver lace to distinguish it, Prussian hussars had dolmans and pelisses in various colours, corded in either white or yellow with different colours of fur for the pelisses. For example, in 1806 the 4th *Regiment Prinz Eugen von Wurttemberg* had a light-blue dolman with a red collar, white frogging and light-blue fur to the pelisse, while the 1st *Regiment von Gettkandt* had a dark-green dolman with a red collar and white frogging and with dark-green fur to the pelisse. The reforms of 1843 did little to affect the hussar dress and it was not until 1860 that a tunic was adopted, sparingly frogged compared with the old style and with five rows in place of the fifteen odd rows of three buttons (Plate 6).

The hussars continued to wear their combination of colours for dolman and pelisse with either white or yellow frogging for other ranks, silver or gold for officers, until the end of full dress. Pelisses usually matched the *attila* for both officers and other ranks except for the *Leib-Garde Hussar* regiment and the 3rd Hussar regiment who wore blue pelisses with red *attilas*. In 1910 the field-grey service dress-jacket issued was cut in exactly the same style and shape as the full dress *attila* with five rows of drab lace on the front, piping along the back seams with a button on the back at the waist; from the end of each seam fell three cords which were knotted at the end. By this time the toggles on the tunics or *attilas* were in metal which matched the lace or cord colour adorning the uniform. In the 1910 field service dress they were dull grey metal.

Lancers too followed the fairly universal style of dress worn in other armies, based on the Polish uniform with a short double-breasted coat with lapels buttoned back forming a plastron.

In 1815 lancers wore an entirely blue uniform with leather protections on the inside of the legs of the overalls which had the usual buttons on

35

the outside seam. The coat was double-breasted with high 'Prussian' collar open at the front to show the neck cloth. The collar, epaulette straps and pointed cuffs were in the regimental facing colour. One main difference in the appearance of the line *Uhlans* from the *Garde Uhlan Regiment* was that the former wore shakos. By the early 1820s, however, lance caps were in use by the line regiments who had now slightly altered their appearance by adopting epaulettes in place of the shoulder straps. The buttons on the outside of the overalls had also disappeared and a cloth stripe had been introduced.

Like the hussars, the lancers did not follow the Prussian trend in 1843 of adopting a tunic, continuing with the coat which was worn for parade wear with a false plastron in the facing colour buttoned on the chest. In 1853 a specially designed tunic termed a *ulanka* was introduced for lancers which was in dark blue with a collar and pointed cuff, and piping on sleeves, back seams, down the leading edge and on the false side in the regimental face colour. The double-breasted *ulanka* was supplied with a cloth plastron which could be buttoned on for full dress wear. The trousers were grey with a red stripe down the outer seam and reinforced with leather. In 1870 breeches and knee boots replaced this nether wear. The appearance of the lancer in the Prussian and later Imperial army remained unaltered until the end of full dress; the button-on plastron and slip-on lance-cap cover in the regimental colours being reserved for full dress.

In 1910 a version of the field uniform was issued modelled on the full dress *ulanka* and piped in the same manner in the regimental facing colour. However, all individuality in style of cut disappeared after 1915 when the *bluse* was issued.

In Sweden uniforms had followed the Prussian style from 1845 and the Royal Horse Guard took to the new Prussian *ulanka* as soon as it appeared in the Prussian army. Plate 75 shows the style of uniform that was being used in 1860 when the Prussian helmet had been replaced by a shako. Plate 76 shows a trooper of the Life Guard Hussar Corps in the 1870 pattern of dress with frogged *attila* and *pelisse* and wearing a short 'kepi' styled head-dress. In 1910, following the lead of Prussia, the Swedish army adopted an entirely grey uniform.

In Denmark the various regimental arrangements and variations in uniforms were abandoned in 1842 when red was adopted by the entire army, cavalry excepted, regimental distinctions being by means of numerals on the shoulder straps. In 1848 a dark blue double-breasted 'frock' type uniform was introduced with red collar patches and piping for infantry and crimson for dragoons and artillery. In 1854 dragoons were ordered a pale blue tunic and an 'Austrian' style helmet was introduced. Plates 77 to 83 show a variety of Danish uniforms of different dates while Plates 84 to 88 show a selection of Austrian infantry and cavalry at various periods, space not permitting a detailed look at these and other countries.

In 1849 white coatees gave way for the Austrian infantry to a double-breasted tunic in the same colour but after Austria's defeat at the hands of the Prussians in 1866 a new dark blue uniform tunic was introduced with regiments being distinguished by the colour of collar and cuffs. For field wear, at the same time, blouses were introduced. Plate 87 shows an infantryman of 1900. In 1909 a field uniform was introduced in grey with the tunic cut similar to the blouse. Dragoons had worn pale blue tunics and pelisses and red breeches and boots from 1868 and they continued to use this uniform up until the First World War when, like the French dragoons, they condescended to place a cover over the helmet before taking the field. At the end of 1914 the red breeches were withdrawn and grey ones issued. Later the pale blue tunics and pelisses were taken away and grey blouses and pelisses issued.

United States of America

(a) INFANTRY

The forces involved on the colonist side against the British troops during the American War of Independence were dressed in a variety of colours, although the style conformed to that worn by the regular British army. A unique colour was selected for the coat which was then further embellished with coloured collar, lapels and cuffs as well as turnbacks. For officers there was always the added distinction of lace, either silver or gold, which was matched by the colour of the buttons. The militia of North America who constituted part of Washington's troops were formed in the American Colonies from early times; they wore no basic uniform colour, each unit being allowed to choose its own colour. In 1775 Congress decided that a brown uniform coat should be introduced as this was the easiest colour of cloth to obtain in sufficient quantity. The differing shades of brown that persisted in the army were due to the fact that the cloth was locally made and therefore no two units wore the same; this is similar to the later adoption of khaki in the British army during the mutiny where locally dyed whites always varied in tone. However, brown was not the universal colour. The New York Infantry in 1775 were noted as wearing coats in blue, dark blue, grey and dark brown while in Connecticut red was a popular colour. In Pennsylvania brown and blue with various facing colours were worn by the infantry.

In 1779 when events had been somewhat rationalised, Washington persuaded Congress to establish a standard system of clothing for the　37 army. In October 1779 it was established that all infantry should wear blue coats and that the colours of the collar and facings should be:

New Hampshire, Massachusetts, Rhode Island, Connecticut—White
Pennsylvania, Delaware, Maryland, Virginia—Red
North Carolina, South Carolina, Georgia—Blue, with white lace button-holes
New York, New Jersey—Buff

This system lasted only until 1782 when red facings were universally designated to all infantry regiments. The nether wear was first of all breeches with stockings but these were soon replaced by overalls which buttoned below the knee on each side giving the appearance of breeches and gaiters in one. The marines wore green uniforms with red facings but in 1797 adopted the infantry blue.

In common with the world-wide evolution in the design of infantry uniforms, the Americans adopted the single-breasted short-tailed coat with laced collar and slashed-flap cuff in dark blue with light-blue trousers. As with the head-dress this probably owed much to the strong, French influence on American uniforms that persisted during the nineteenth century. In undress wear, infantry were issued with a short, shell jacket in the same colour as the trousers with a high, open, laced collar and devoid of any ornamentation on the cuffs.

In 1851 a frock-type tunic was introduced for the infantry and continued in wear until the American Civil War. Epaulettes were added for rank and file in 1855 of plain metal scales rather than the worsted ones worn previously. The 1864 regulations describe the uniforms as:

. . . single-breasted frock, of dark blue cloth, made without plaits, with a skirt extending one-half the distance from the top of the hip to the bend of the knee; one row nine buttons on the breast, placed at equal distances; stand collar, to rise no higher than to permit the chin to turn freely over it, . . . cuffs pointed according to pattern, and to button with two small buttons at the under seam; collar and cuffs edged with cord of welt of cloth as follows, to wit: Scarlet for *Artillery*; sky blue for *infantry*; yellow for *Engineers*; crimson for *Ordnance and Hospital Stewards* . . . pockets in the folds of the skirts, with one button at each hip to range with the lowest button on the breast.

Officers of all ranks were ordered a dark blue coat of the same style to be single-breasted for captains and lieutenants but double-breasted for other ranks. Major-generals had buttons placed in threes, while brigadier-generals wore them in pairs; colonels wore them singly. The most popular dress, especially during the Civil War, was the prescribed fatigue dress:

> a sack coat of dark blue flannel extending half-way down to the thigh and made loose without sleeve or body lining; falling collar, inside pocket on the left side, four coat buttons down the front.

By 1864 the trousers worn were in dark blue cloth, 'without plaits and to spread well over the boot' except for the artillery who wore sky-blue. Each arm of the service was distinguished by trouser stripes, sergeants and corporals of infantry having stripes of differing widths in the colour of the corps which were: yellow for cavalry, scarlet for artillery and sky-blue for infantry. Privates wore plain trousers.

During the American Civil War the southern States adopted grey as their uniform colour, but cut in a similar style to that of the northern troops. Both sides had volunteers dressed exactly in the same manner as the French 'Zouaves', Duryea's Zouves in the North having red trousers, blue jackets with red tape and sky-blue cummerbund while Hawkins' Zouves wore dark blue trousers, dark blue jackets and vests with a red 'fez'. In the Confederate army 'zouave' regiments were also employed, the Louisiana Zouaves having red trousers and dark blue jackets with a red 'fez'. The style was identical to the French pattern with baggy trousers tucked into fawn leggings and short white spats.

In 1872 a shorter, blue tunic was introduced for the infantry, with collar patches on which was placed the regimental number. The tunic was single-breasted and had a slashed-flap cuff. Epaulettes had disappeared and shoulder straps in the same colour as the collar patch were worn. In 1881, when the felt helmet was introduced, the tunic altered in having the entire collar in the facing colour. In 1884 the infantry colour which had up until this date been light or sky blue was changed to white, but in 1902 the whole conception was changed again and pale blue given to the infantry as their facing colour. The tunic which was now adopted for garrison and ceremonial duties was dark blue with light blue piped collar, shoulder straps and round cuff which displayed two buttons, one above the other. The trousers were also light blue. The tunic was adorned with cords and tassels for ceremonial dress and the various corps insignia were worn in brass on the collar: crossed rifles with the regimental and company number for the infantry, and crossed sabres for the cavalry. The letters 'U.S.' were also worn on the collar.

In 1902 khaki field service uniforms were introduced in the American army which for infantry consisted of tunic, breeches and leggings. The same distinctions for officers were worn on the collar but in bronze.

(b) CAVALRY

In 1779, regulations issued for the uniforms of the American army specified white collar, cuffs and lapels for the dragoons who wore a long coat with turned-back skirts and buttoned-back lapels similar to British light dragoons. After the Revolutionary War, dragoons disappeared from the American army and were not brought back until 1833 when they were ordered to wear a dark blue single-breasted jacket with 'Prussian' collar adorned with lace, and pointed cuffs edged in yellow piping. The trousers or overalls were light blue with a broad, yellow stripe. In 1864 the uniform of light dragoons is given in the regulations as:

> *All Enlisted Men of the Cavalry and Light Artillery* shall wear a uniform jacket of dark blue cloth, with one row of twelve buttons on the breast, placed at equal distances; stand up collar . . . to hook over in front at the bottom, and to slope the same as the coat collar; on the collar, on each side two blind button-holes of lace, three-eighths of an inch wide, one small button on the button-hole, lower button-hole extending back four inches, upper button-hole three and a half inches; top button and front edge of collar bound with lace . . . and a strip of the same extending down the front and around the whole lower edge of the jacket; the back seam laced with the same, and on the cuff a point of the same shape as that on the coat but formed of lace . . . colour of lace (worsted), yellow for *Cavalry*, and scarlet for *Light Artillery*.

Trousers were dark blue except for the light artillery which wore light blue, those of the mounted men being reinforced with leather.

After the American Civil War the cavalry too adopted a tunic and wore it until the demise of full dress. Blouses were supplied for campaign wear, officers wearing double-breasted versions on occasions piped in yellow or white. In 1902 the cavalry succumbed to the influence of khaki and adopted a field service dress with shirt, breeches and boots, which were worn in Cuba at the turn of the century. By the time of the American entry into the First World War the cavalry uniform was the same as that of the infantry, the only means of distinguishing them being the collar badges.

Infantry and cavalry uniforms are in modern armies today barely distinguishable one from another, but differences can be seen in the full or parade dress occasionally worn. From 'uniform' beginnings at the end of the seventeenth century when dress was similar because of cost, the various armies and arms of the army have progressed and diversified in colour and cut to suit their own purposes only to return after over 200 years to the almost identical state of affairs of the late 1600s. Modern warfare now makes no concession for individual corps insignia or traditional trappings, and every item of clothing or equipment carried or worn by the soldier has a practical use. Only in ceremonial dress is there room for sentimentality and for the insignia and dress of another era when camouflage was insignificant and colours of uniforms all important to an army taking the field.

2 : Head-dress 1740–1918

In 1740, at the time of the outbreak of the War of the Austrian Succession, the majority of the soldiery, both infantry and cavalry of the armies involved (Austria, Great Britain, Netherlands and Russia against Prussia, Bavaria, France, Spain and Sweden) were wearing a hat with the brim turned up on three sides, similar to that in vogue with civilians.

The hat, which had replaced the steel pikeman's pot in the armies of Europe, was at first worn with the right side turned up and held in position by a loop of lace or, in some armies, a badge, emblem, feather or cockade in national colours. In England this was known as the 'Monmouth cock'. The accession to the throne by William of Orange brought to England the Dutch fashion of cocking the hat on both sides; by the beginning of the eighteenth century the back was also turned up to form the well-known tricorn hat. The shape of the tricorn hat varied from army to army or as one fashion ousted another. There were also many varied additions such as cockades in leather or silk, feathers, plumes and badges or emblems denoting the country of the wearer. In order to strengthen the hat, which was of fairly poor quality material, the edge of the brim was bound in tape which was usually black, yellow or white.

In Britain the 'Ramillies cock' was adopted after the battle of that name but by 1751 it had been replaced by the 'Dettingen cock'. By 1756 the fashion seems to have been for hats to be 'cocked in the Cumberland manner'. The most important consideration, however, appears to have been that uniformity was maintained as the following order from the 'Regimental Order Book' of the British 2nd Dragoons shows:

22ND JAN. 1759. A stiver to be stopt from each man for having his hatt cocked, which the Major hopes the men won't be against paying as it is for their own advantage.

However, three days later, a further order added that,

. . . no man to presume to alter the cock otherwise it will be done over again & he be obliged to pay every time it is not in shape.

In 1766 the French ambassador to England introduced the 'Nivernois cock' which was a small hat with the flaps fastened up with hooks and eyes, but by 1775 the fashion had once more changed. In the 'Clothing Warrant of 1768' the hats are described as follows:

> The Hats of the Serjeants to be laced with Silver. Those of the Corporals and Private Men, to have a White Tape Binding. The Breadth of the Whole to be one Inch and a Quarter; and no more to be on the Back Part of the Brim, than what is necessary to sew it down. To have Black Cockades.

In the cavalry the hats were laced in gold or silver for the officers and yellow or white for the men.

Towards the end of the eighteenth century, the front point had become a small spout and the brim turned up almost flat. In the last decade of the eighteenth century the cocked hat started to disappear and was finally replaced by a cylindrical cap termed a shako or 'chaco'; however, the cavalry whose hat had now become almost a 'bicorn' continued to wear it until a helmet in one form or another ousted it.

In America the Regulations of 30th January 1787 detailed that the hat, which was worn by infantry as well as artillery, should be

> ... cocked with white trimming for infantry and yellow for artillery.

The cockades were 'black leather, round with points, four inches diameter . . . the feathers to rise six inches above the brim of the hat'. A complicated system of coloured feathers was used in America as well as other countries. The artillery had black with a red top, while the three regiments of infantry had red, black and white respectively. In Britain the plume was white on red for battalion company men, the flank companies wearing caps of a particular design. On the Continent the Bavarian Guard wore a blue, white and black plume, while the French during the revolution tended to favour the national colours. Perhaps the most complicated was the system used in Sweden which consisted of a vertical feather on the left side as a national emblem and the crown covered in feathers of various colours denoting the regiment or formation.

The cocked hat lingered on for general officers and others in many armies, cavalry officers wearing an exaggerated form known as a 'chapeaux bras' with levee dress and court dress. It is still in use today and can be seen at ceremonial parades, although the height has diminished somewhat from the lavish versions of the 1830s.

Besides the cocked hat, there was another form of head-dress at the beginning of the eighteenth century which was worn by grenadiers, men trained in the art of throwing grenades. As they were required to sling their muskets over their shoulders before beginning the drill for lighting and throwing the grenade the tricorn hat would have been a hindrance. In its place these selected troops wore a cap which varied to a considerable extent within Europe.

Grenadiers were first introduced in Britain in the 1670s and the cap worn by these new troops was described by the diarist Evelyn when he witnessed a review on Hounslow Heath in June 1678. He described the men as wearing,

> '. . . furred caps with coped crowns like Janizaries which made them look very fierce and some had long hoods hanging down behind as we picture fools.'

The fur cap soon disappeared and a cap with a raised, stiffened, cloth front took its place. This front was a convenient place to display the crest of the Sovereign or the colonel of the regiment. By the end of the reign of Queen Anne the hanging bag at the back was also stiffened thus forming the 'mitre cap'.

The continental counterpart of this cap varied to a great extent. The Prussians and the Russians usually had a metal front embossed with designs including cyphers etc while the Austrians continued with a fur cap which had a stiffened, pointed front displaying a metal plate, and a bag of cloth ornamented with a tassel. The Prussian artillery adopted a grenadier-type cap in 1731 which was a round reinforced cap with a higher metal plate at the front. This pattern was copied by other Prussian regiments with the round cap in various coloured cloths. It is from this basic style with a metal front that a number of head-dresses were evolved, and adopted by light cavalry.

In 1768 British grenadiers adopted in place of the cloth cap a stiffened fur cap with metal plate at the front and grenade at the back. The fur cap had been worn previously by some regiments, notably the 42nd Royal Highlanders. In Europe, other countries clung to the old style grenadier cap of stiffened cloth with embroidered cloth or metal front, Prussia and Russia being the most faithful to the metal-fronted cap which endured in both armies until 1914, while France and various German States such as Baden, Italy and Spain adopted the fur cap. Except for Prussia, Russia and countries under their sphere of influence in uniform matters, the trend of other countries was to develop the fur cap. It became larger as the nineteenth century progressed, losing in many countries the ornamental plate and, after the demise of grenadier companies, becoming the head-dress of certain élite troops. Today it is still worn by the British Foot Guards and was, up until 1914 and the twilight of full dress, worn by the Royal Scots Greys who from an early period had adopted a grenadier 'mitre cap' in one form or another. The Royal Life Guards of Denmark also still wear the fur cap but nearer to its original form with chin scales, tassels and a plate bearing the national arms on the front. The fur cap was adopted in 1803 and the plate added in 1842.

Another form of cap was adopted in various countries by light companies or light infantry. This usually took the form of a strengthened, leather, round cap, similar to that adopted by the Prussian artillery. It had a crest to which was fitted a plume of horsehair, and a raised metal pointed front which was used to display emblems and badges. The style was very similar to that adopted in some countries by light dragoons. In Britain various light companies adopted this form of cap, that of the 5th Foot having a gosling-green turban wound around the base and a pointed blackened metal plate at the front bearing badges and devices. With the arrival of the shako most light infantry or light companies, unlike grenadiers who clung to their particular style of cap, adopted the shako with a distinctive plume or badge to denote their role.

Turning to the cavalry, the cocked hat was a popular head-dress after the 'lobster tail' helmet was discarded, but fur-trimmed caps similar to that first adopted by grenadiers seem to have been favoured in some countries. In England horse grenadiers adopted the grenadier cap as being more practical in battle, while other regiments of dragoons, who often had to sling their muskets to be able to use their swords, found the round cap of reinforced leather or cloth with a stiffened cloth of metal front more practical. In Britain all except the Royal North British Dragoons (in 1877 the Royal Scots Greys and now the Royal Scots Dragoon Guards) wore the cap. The Scots Greys adopted a grenadier-styled cap and in 1768 when the fur cap came into use they adopted this model and retained a fur cap, in one form or another, in full dress until 1914. The regiment, it appears, still retained the hat for other than full-dress wear, as an extract from the following order shows (June 1779):

> . . . The men to march out of Quarters in their New Cap, but when they return swords, they are to put their Hats on, and wrap their Caps in a Handkerchief to prevent them from being Dusted.

In European armies the dragoons wore either the cocked hat edged in tape with a cockade and plume in the national or regimental colours, the mitre-shaped cap or, in the case of one French regiment, a metal helmet with a crest and animal-skin band. This pattern with the addition of back and front peaks was to form the basis for the French cavalry helmet until 1918.

Light cavalry in the form of hussars copied from the Hungarian light cavalry was first formed in Prussia in 1721 and twenty years later was enlarged in number by Frederick the Great. Unlike other regiments of hussars which copied the national costume and fur cap of the Hungarian hussars, the Von Rueesch Hussar Regiment adopted a black uniform, 45 death's-head and crossed bones badge, and a tall cylindrical cloth cap with a pennon-styled tail known as a mirliton or *Flugelmutze*. The French who had hussars as early as 1701 also adopted the mirliton in 1752, this form of head-dress also being taken into wear by Russian regiments. Britain only formed, or converted, existing light cavalry regiments into hussars at the beginning of the nineteenth century when they wore a fur hat named a 'kalpak' but in England termed a busby, probably after a certain W. Busby, a hatter with a shop in the Strand, London.

Light cavalry, formed in Britain as light squadrons attached to dragoon and dragoon guard regiments in 1755, were authorised in 1756 to wear 'jockey leather caps with the Royal Cypher and Crown in brass in front and also the rank of the regiment'. The successful use of these light cavalry troops persuaded the authorities to form five regiments of light dragoons in 1759 and two more the following year. The new regiments continued to wear caps, but in various styles. All conformed to the round hat with turned-up front peak which displayed the Royal Cypher and regimental distinctions, and a crest which sported a horsehair plume. The 15th Light Dragoons had a particularly attractive and decorative helmet with a metal skull, while other regiments favoured leather with reinforced bars on the side.

By the early 1780s this style had been replaced by a leather helmet with peak, surmounted by a bearskin or fur crest. By 1788 the five existing regiments of light dragoons with the exception of the 15th were wearing this pattern. In France it was adopted by *Chasseurs à cheval* in 1789 who retained it in certain regiments until the early 1800s while others adopted the mirliton around 1796. In Britain it continued in use until 1812 for regular regiments, although some yeomanry and the Royal Horse Artillery wore it up until 1827. In 1796 another version of the helmet 'made of tin and lined with white linen to repel the effects of the sun' was authorised for light dragoons in hot climates.

Versions of the 'Tarleton' helmet with fur crest were worn in many countries. The infantry and cavalry of Bavaria adopted it to some extent and certain regiments of Danish light dragoons adopted it in 1794 with a distinctive elongated fur crest at the back which extended to the base of the jacket collar. The Hanoverian horse artillery also wore this pattern of head-dress and it continued in Bavaria until the late nineteenth century in a much modified form with a diminutive crest.

The last distinctive style of head-dress, faithfully copied by nearly every army that had lancers, was the *czapka*, from the Polish meaning 'a cap'. It was developed from the traditional and national cap called a *konfederatka* which had a squared top and which continued in the Polish army until 1918 almost in its original form. The cap was developed by the lancers in 1798 with the addition of a peak. The Austrians had regular lancer regiments by 1791, the French adopting this form of light cavalry in 1807 when Polish lancers entered Napoleon's army. The British did not form lancer regiments until 1816 when some light dragoon regiments were converted to this new role. The Russians too had a regiment of Polish lancers wearing the distinctive cap but the bulk of their light cavalry was made up of hussars wearing the mirliton, and cossacks who wore a distinctive dress with a small round cap or fur 'kalpak'. The latter were probably the finest light cavalry troops in the world.

Britain

(a) INFANTRY

The first shako worn by the British infantry was authorised on 24th February 1800 and was a cylindrical cap of lacquered leather with a peak. Known as a 'stovepipe' because of its shape, the front of the cap bore a brass plate embossed with a crowned garter and motto; inside was the cypher G.R. This central design was superimposed on a trophy of flags and arms with the lion of England positioned beneath the garter. The black leather cockade at the top centre was fitted behind with a plume: white on red for battalion companies, green for light companies and white for grenadiers who on occasion replaced their fur caps with the shako. In 1806 a felt version was ordered but in 1811 a Board of General Officers claimed that the stovepipe shako was 'objectionable as to form, unsteady on the head, little use against the weather or sword cuts' and ordered a new pattern to be adopted. This was approved on 24th December 1811 and taken into wear in 1812. It was of black felt with a false front on which the badge was fitted, a black leather peak, and a plume fitted in a black rosette on the left side. Plaited, white (gold for officers) cap lines were fitted at each side and hung down over the peak. A Horse Guards circular of February 1812 permitted the use of badges or regimental number on the plate while an order of December 1814 stated that 'Corps of Rifles and Light Infantry and Light Companies . . . shall have a bugle horn with the number of the regiment below it, instead of a brass plate'.

The cap was expected to last two years. It had been considered that an iron plate should be supplied as protection against sword blows but it was felt that 'the soldier carrying his forage cap in the vacancy of his regimental cap' was sufficiently protected; and in any case the iron, if wet, would rust and ruin the felt of the shako. The Portuguese had adopted a similar shako in 1806 with a false front and the Austrian infantry had been wearing a peakless leather cap with false front since 47

1769; with its brass plate it was strangely similar to that adopted for the British shako. The rifles and light infantry, however, continued with the stovepipe shako.

During the occupation of Paris after the battle of Waterloo, the flamboyant head-dresses of the Prussians and Austrians were soon noted by the British, resulting in a new, Prussian-style shako being ordered for the British infantry and artillery. The new shako authorised in August 1815 was $7\frac{1}{2}$ inches high, eleven inches in diameter, with a large top and tapering towards the head band. The top and bottom of the shako were bound in lace with a circular plate on the front. The plume increased in height to twelve inches, making the shako most imposing. This shape, the 'bell top', continued in use with modifications until the introduction of a cylindrical shako, said to be designed by Prince Albert, in 1844. In 1828 the lace on the shako gave way to black leather, the height was lowered to six inches and a large star plate introduced. In 1835 the plume gave way to a ball tuft, following the change in other European countries. Cap lines, introduced with the shako, were abandoned in 1830.

The 'Albert' shako introduced in 1844 probably took its inspiration from the cylindrical French pattern approved for the infantry in 1837 in answer to the demand for a lighter and more practical head-dress. The new shako, $6\frac{1}{4}$ inches high, measured $6\frac{1}{4}$ inches across the black leather top. The body was made of felt and on the front bore a star plate surmounted by a crown. There were two peaks, one at the front and a smaller one at the rear, similar to those fitted on Austrian shakos since 1806. Chin chains were fitted to each side by rosettes. There was a leather chin strap for the rank and file who since 1839 had worn a round shako plate surmounted by a crown with the regimental number in the centre.

Fusiliers, who had worn a fur cap previously, and grenadier companies adopted the shako with a white ball tuft and a grenade badge; rifle and light companies wore a green ball tuft.

Being allied with the French during the Crimean War brought the British army once again in contact with continental fashions, which in 1855 resulted in the British copying the French pattern of shako which was lower and tilted forward, and shaped to the head at the rear. Up until this date the officers' shako plates had been particularly handsome, incorporating a scroll with honours, wreaths and other decorations; but in 1855 the new, smaller shako gave no scope for an elaborate badge, and a small star plate with the regimental number inside the Garter on a black leather ground was adopted. Some regiments managed to incorporate one or more battle honours.

48   The artillery, who had followed the infantry in choice of head-dress,

4. *Panel made from the base drum of the Royal Inniskilling Fusiliers circa 1870*

5. *Pipe banner of the Royal Scots Fusiliers circa 1926.*

6. *Officer's pouches, left to right: Heavy Cavalry circa 1860, 9th Lancers special regimental pattern circa 1850*

7. *Lt-Colonel, A.D.C. to William IV circa 1835*

8. *Silver epaulette of a British Lord Lieutenant*

9. *Queen Victoria's Christmas chocolate box 1900; discharge papers and medal of Private Hawkins of the Wiltshire Regiment*

adopted the busby in 1855 with a brass grenade on the left side displaying the Royal Arms, field gun and mottoes of the regiment as well as serving as a holder for a white plume. As with the light cavalry and horse artillery busby from which it was copied, it had a cloth bag hanging down on the right side.

Other regiments not wearing the shako were those on the Highland establishment with the exception of the 71st who, being light infantry, wore a shako but with a diced band. The Highlanders wore the feather bonnet with a diced band and a regimental badge fitted on a black rosette on the left side. Behind the badge was fitted a plume, white for all with the exception of the 42nd Black Watch who wore a red hackle awarded to them for distinguished conduct in 1793.

The new shako, ornamented in the Austrian manner around the top with bands of gold lace (silver for militia) to denote field officers, continued until 1860 when a lower version of the same shape was ordered. This departed from previous patterns in being made of cloth with lines of stitching on those of the officers. Light infantry and light companies received permission to wear a green drooping plume in obvious emphasis of their dashing role. The shako was authorised in November 1860, some eight months after the French adopted the shako on which the design was based.

The plate continued to be in the form of a small star with regimental numeral, and officers of field rank continued the custom of having bands of gold lace around the top. In 1869 another version lower in height but of the same shape was authorised. It was in blue cloth for the infantry and green with a black ball tuft for the light infantry; royal regiments and the 46th were ordered an all-red ball tuft. This pattern had the distinction of gold lace around the crown, the bottom and down the side seams, with a new style plate, and a return to the chin chain which had been abandoned in 1855. The Highland Light Infantry (71st, 74th) and 91st had their distinctive shako with diced band and black corded lines above the peak.

The resounding defeat of the French by the Prussians in 1870 led, eight years later, to the shako being abandoned, except for the 71st, 74th and 91st in the British army. The natural source for the new head-dress design was the victor over a nation which had dictated the fashion for some thirty years. Prussia soon re-united with other German States to form the German Empire.

The helmet, introduced in May 1878, was destined for all infantry, artillery, corps and departments; and at one time even the highland regiments wearing their bonnets were almost ordered the helmet. The larger area of the front heralded the return of the large star plate, with the Garter in the centre, the regimental number and, in some cases, 49 honours. This numbered badge gave way to a territorial badge when the infantry regiments were linked into two battalion regiments under a territorial title in 1881.

In 1892 the rifles abandoned the helmet in favour of a busby with small badge on the front and plume, and at the same time the Scottish Rifles adopted a green cloth shako shaped like that of the Highland Light Infantry. The helmet came in a variety of colours and metal fittings. The body was covered most commonly in dark blue for infantry, artillery, corps, etc; dark green for rifles (up until 1892), a lighter green for light infantry and a multitude of shades of grey for volunteers. The metal fittings were brass for the infantry, silver for militia and some volunteers and bronze for rifles and other volunteers.

In 1904 two Scottish lowland regiments abandoned the helmet and adopted the new style 'Kilmarnock' bonnet which had a slanted top, diced band and plume of cockerel's feathers on the right side.

Even after 1918, when full dress was not generally insisted on, the Royal Artillery in 1928 managed to justify a change back to the busby abandoned in 1878. Fusiliers, who since the early 1860s had worn their own pattern of fur cap, were not affected by any subsequent change in head-dress.

(b) CAVALRY

In 1812 the Household Cavalry were ordered a helmet in place of the cocked hat although the Royal Horse Guards did not receive theirs until 1814. At the same time, the heavy cavalry of dragoons and dragoon guards were also ordered a helmet. This new style, based on the Austrian helmet, had a leather skull with a brass-bound peak and a brass crest with 'Medusa' head sporting a typically French horsehair tuft and mane. The lower edge was bound with brass scales and the plate, rising to meet the crest, was embossed with the crown over the intertwined and reversed Royal Cypher above an oval bearing the title of the regiment. In 1814 the Household Cavalry abandoned the horse-hair tuft and mane and substituted a crest in red and blue worsted; a white over red plume was added to the left side, the straight peak became downward-pointing and the regimental designation in the oval was dispensed with.

In 1818 the heavy cavalry adopted a helmet based on that ordered for the Household Cavalry the previous year, with a different colour of skull and peak. That of the Household Cavalry was polished steel with brass fittings while the heavy cavalry helmet was black with brass fittings. The crest on the top of the helmet was, in both cases, of bearskin and the whole looked somewhat difficult to maintain in position when at a trot or gallop. Nevertheless, this form of head-dress lasted until 1842 in the Household Cavalry and until 1834 in the heavy cavalry.

The Household Cavalry adopted a tall bearskin cap with '. . . the Royal Arms and other devices and having a white plume of feathers on the left side passing in a circular direction over the crown of the cap'. The helmet as previously described seems also to have been worn on occasion until 1833 when a new pattern fur cap superseded all other head-dress.

In 1834 the heavy cavalry were ordered a new pattern helmet which had a brass skull, a peak and foliages. In undress the front of the crest was fitted with a lion head but in full dress the fur crest employed on the previous pattern was utilised. The rayed plate bearing the Royal Coat of Arms and battle honours was fitted above a head band which bore the number and title of the regiment.

Fourteen years later, in 1843, a simplified version of the helmet was ordered. While being basically the same shape, the removal of the decoration of the skull and the substitution of a horsehair mane and tuft similar to the 1812 helmet made this head-dress particularly ugly and unattractive. It was in use for only three years and examples are extremely rare to find.

It is difficult to understand why the heavy cavalry did not adopt the helmet approved for the Household Cavalry in 1842. Copied from Russian and Prussian metal helmets, it had a skull of simpler proportions with a smaller badge; and in the place of the crest, a foliage-fluted brass point held the horsehair plume. In 1847, however, the heavy cavalry followed the lead of the three senior cavalry regiments and adopted a white metal helmet with brass fittings for the two regiments of dragoons (the Royal Scots Greys had by this time adopted a bearskin cap) and an all brass helmet for the dragoon guards. By 1855 various colours of plume were used to distinguish one regiment from another: King's Dragoon Guards (1st), red; 2nd Dragoon Guards (Bays), black; 3rd Dragoon Guards (Carabiniers), black and red; 4th Dragoon Guards, white; 5th Dragoon Guards, red and white; 6th Dragoon Guards, black; 7th Dragoon Guards, black and white; 1st Dragoons wore black and the 6th wore white.

In 1871 the helmet for both Household Cavalry and heavy cavalry was simplified by the removal of the skull and peak foliage and the adoption, except for the Household Cavalry, of a new star plate and the substitution of a tapered four-sided plume holder for the foliage version of the 'Albert' helmet. The plume colours remained the same until the post 1914–18 war amalgamation when the 3/6th Dragoon Guards wore black and red; the 4/7th, white; and the 5th Dragoon

Guards amalgamated with the 6th Dragoons had red and white, but retained the white metal helmet of the 6th.

The light cavalry had by the early 1800s been divided into three distinctively dressed arms and it is preferable that they be treated separately. The light dragoons had, in 1812, given up their fur-crested 'Tarleton' style helmets and adopted a bell-top shako copied from the contemporary Austrian cap. The similarity in silhouette between the new shakos and that of the French caused some anxious moments during the Peninsular War. In common with the shako, it was copied from the new light dragoon pattern and had a plain leather peak at the front and a wider leather peak at the back which could be turned up flush against the helmet when not in use. The top of the cap was ornamented in lace or braid, with a boss or rosette in the centre to hold the white-over-red plume. The design on the front of the shako was in nearly all cases a 'wheel' made up of lace or braid, with a regimental button in the centre. Chin scales were fitted each side and the shako fitted with cap lines to prevent loss in action, the head-dress being a costly part of the uniform paid for by the soldier himself.

1822 heralded a more ornate and more bell-shaped shako for the remaining light dragoons (hussars and lancers had been formed prior to this date). The general appearance, except for the richer embellishment and exaggerated plume, was akin to the infantry whom the light dragoons followed in shako styles until their disappearance in 1861. A more ornate shako with a distinctive 'Maltese Cross' shako plate was adopted in 1830 with chin chains, large feather plume, ornate cap lines and flounders which were fitted over the peak before being fitted over the body of the wearer. By 1840, however, the heavy festooning over the peak was discontinued.

Light dragoons were ordered a new pattern shako in common with the infantry in 1844. It followed the 'Albert' infantry pattern in shape, except that it had a flare at the top, and had a gold embroidered front peak, lace around the top, no back peak and a 'Maltese Cross' style plate. Oilskin covers were worn in wet weather and white quilted covers in tropical climates, but both these items are almost impossible to find as the ravages of active service and age have taken a heavy toll. This is also probably true of other ranks' items which, although less desirable and lower-priced than officers' items, are on the whole much scarcer.

Between 1855 and 1857 a new shako was adopted by the light dragoons, modelled once more on the infantry pattern but with the 'Maltese Cross' plate and a band of lace around the top. Finally in 1861, the last traces of the old-fashioned light dragoons vanished when the existing regiments were converted to hussars, adopting their distinctive dress and fur busby.

Hussars first appeared in the British army in 1805 when the 7th, 10th, 15th and 18th Light Dragoons were converted into hussars. At first, the regiments adopted a cylindrical shako and the mirliton copied from their continental counterparts but by 1807 they had adopted the 'monstrous muffs' ornamented with a scarlet cloth bag on the right side, the 18th being alone in favouring a blue bag. As with other light dragoon head-dress, cap lines were worn to prevent loss in action, but even so the fur cap was rejected in most regiments by 1809 as being too fragile against the elements. In accord with their dashing rakish appearance, hussars were not ones to be governed too strictly by regulations when it came to the sartorial elegance of high fashion. A variety of shakos were worn in varying colours of cloth, the 15th having scarlet as well as the 10th, the latter retaining it until 1855.

In 1841 the 11th Hussars adopted, or re-adopted, the busby with their own special crimson bag. This led to other regiments gradually abandoning the shako for the 'monstrous muff' which had been somewhat streamlined since that remark was passed. All other hussar regiments had a scarlet cloth bag which in 1855 was ornamented with gold, Russian braid. The plume, in varying colours, denoted the regiment. In 1864 the increase in the number of hussar regiments by the conversion of remaining light dragoons and inclusion of three regiments from the old East India Company armies brought a variety of coloured bags and plumes.

Regiment	Busby bag	Plume
3rd Hussars	Garter blue	White
4th Hussars	Yellow	Scarlet
7th Hussars	Scarlet	White
10th Hussars	Scarlet	Black and white
11th Hussars	Crimson	Crimson and white
13th Hussars	Buff	White
14th Hussars	Yellow	White
15th Hussars	Scarlet	Scarlet
18th Hussars	Green	Green
19th Hussars	White	White
20th Hussars	Crimson	Crimson
21st Hussars	French grey	White

By 1883 the 18th had adopted a blue bag and scarlet and white plume, and in 1892 the 20th adopted an all-yellow plume.

The height of the busby was reduced in 1888 to $6\frac{1}{4}$ inches in front and $7\frac{3}{4}$ inches at the back and in 1891 the plume was increased to thirteen inches. There were also other regimental peculiarities which are worth noting: the 15th had no lines around the busby and the 7th did not loop the body lines up on the chest, placing them only around the neck.

Besides the regular army, there were a large number of yeomanry regiments who wore the busby usually with silver lace on the bag and a silver corded boss, chin chains and plume holder. The Yorkshire Hussars had the distinction of having the boss on the busby in scarlet cloth embroidered with the Prince of Wales's feathers while the other ranks had a white metal rose boss. Other ranks replaced the gold lace and gilt fittings with yellow worsted cord and brass.

The Royal Horse Artillery adopted the busby in 1827 and continued with it until the demise of full dress. It is still worn today by the King's Troop, Royal Horse Artillery on ceremonial occasions. The bag was always scarlet and plain and the plume all white.

Lancers were formed in Britain in 1816 when four regiments of light dragoons, 9th, 12th, 16th and 23rd were converted. The 23rd were disbanded the following year, its place being taken by the 19th who suffered the same fate in 1821. The following year the 17th Light Dragoons took its place as a lancer regiment.

The first pattern cap was almost a direct copy of the continental cap and, perhaps more noticeably, the French cap. The almost straight-sided cap with flared, square top was ornamented on the top left with a boss in looped, gold wire to hold the plume. In the centre on velvet was an embroidered royal cypher. The large rayed front plate displayed the royal arms and battle honours, these increasing in number as the century wore on. The peak was in leather and edged in bands of gold lace. A broad band of lace encircled the cap at its waist. At the rear of the cap was a large, plain, black leather peak which could be turned down in inclement weather. This feature figured on all lancer caps up until 1855 although the last pattern had the peak stitched flush to the back of the cap and was incapable of being turned down.

By 1855 the 'waist' was becoming more pronounced and the cap adopted in 1856 had a definite waist, the skull tapering in and then flaring out to the square top. The simple plates of the pre-1856 days were soon forgotten and the new cap plate was heavily ornamented with battle honours, scrolls, leaves and laurels which were in silver on a gilt plate for the officers and stamped in brass for the rank and file.

The 9th Lancers were the exception. In 1832 their special pattern of cap was in black patent leather with black cloth sides to the square leather top and metal fitting in place of lace. In the metal boss, with button in the centre, the regiment wore a black and white plume.

At this period the 12th wore a scarlet plume, the 16th scarlet and white and the 17th all white. The 5th Lancers were created in 1858 and took to wearing a dark green plume to denote the regiment's Irish connections.

A further lancer regiment was added when in 1897 the 21st Hussars were converted. At first they wore a red-topped cap but in 1898 made a return to their particular colour of French grey.

The individual characteristics of each lancer regiment are listed below:

Regiment	Sides and top	Plume	Boss
9th Lancers	Black leather top, cloth sides	Black and and white	Gilt metal
12th Lancers	Scarlet cloth	Scarlet	Gold wire, blue velvet centre
16th Lancers	Black	Black	Scarlet, velvet centre
17th Lancers	White	White	Blue velvet centre
21st Lancers	French grey	White	French grey velvet centre
5th Lancers	Scarlet cloth	Green	Green velvet centre

The 17th had a black plume between 1874 and 1883 while the 16th, who had had scarlet and white, adopted black in 1881.

As with the hussars, there were a number of yeomanry regiments who copied the uniform and cap, each with their distinctive coloured tops and plumes. All except one copied the normal pattern with cloth top; the exception being the Lanarkshire Yeomanry who faithfully copied the 9th Lancer cap, substituting their eagle badge on the plate and their button on the boss. Very few of this pattern were made and it is doubtful whether any other versions were produced for other ranks.

Apart from the 17th, other ranks' lance caps followed those of the officers except that leather tops were fitted in black. The 17th had white leather tops. Instead of gold, except for warrant officers, other ranks had lace in yellow worsted sometimes with a central stripe of regimental pattern. In inclement weather, foul-weather covers were worn over the dress cap without a plume but by the Victorian period officers were having made a special all-leather version of the cap to resemble the foul-weather covering. Regimental distinctions between these caps were omitted, except for the 17th who in place of lion-head, chin-chain bosses wore skull bosses.

Up until the Crimean War soldiers fought in their full dress head-dress but after that date, when much of the fighting was in Africa or India, this was abandoned in favour of the more comfortable and practical forage cap with white cover. The introduction of the white cloth-covered wicker helmet, and in the 1870s the white cloth-covered cork helmet, made this the universal campaign head-dress for the soldier. 55

In India where khaki had gained a foothold, the helmets were worn with a khaki cover. With the introduction of a universal foreign service dress, khaki helmets or white helmets with khaki covers were worn. In South Africa, the British army fighting against the Boers temporarily adopted the bush or slouch hat which was soon abandoned when the war was over. It was, however, favoured more by Colonial and Empire troops and incidentally formed the inspiration for the head-dress adopted by Baden Powell's Boy Scouts.

The lessons learned in the Boer War were speedily digested, resulting in the disappearance, for ever, of the 'red coat' from the field of battle. The uniform for wear at home, except for full dress, was a service dress of khaki with a peaked cap to match. In warmer climates the suit was made of khaki drill and a cloth-covered cork helmet was worn together with such necessary (or so it was said) equipment as a spine pad and cholera belt, not to mention a sun shade fitted to the helmet. In 1916, amidst the fierce and heavy fighting in France, the British army adopted a steel helmet for wear by all arms of the service; the 'Wolseley' cork helmet was reserved for warmer climes. The story of head-dress seems to have turned full circle from the pikeman's pot (abandoned in the seventeenth century) to a great variety of styles until 1916 when a helmet not dissimilar to that of the seventeenth-century pikeman was adopted.

France

(a) INFANTRY

The French army re-organising and recovering from the throes of the French Revolution wore a variety of head-dresses but unlike the sweeping political changes the head-dress remained as it was in the Royalist army. Bearskin caps for grenadiers had been ordered in 1755 and officially sanctioned in 1767, the year before they were generally adopted in Britain but by 1790 the bulk of the infantry were wearing the cocked hat so favoured in France. This penchant for the cocked hat by the new revolutionary country was perhaps one of the strongest reasons for its decline elsewhere. In 1791 the infantry were ordered a helmet based closely on that adopted by the British light dragoons complete with fur crest and turban, known in France as the '*Casque à la Tarleton*'. By 1793, however, very few had been issued and a return was made to the hat for the bulk of the infantry. Grenadiers retained, where supplies permitted, their fur caps first worn in 1755.

To understand the variety of shakos worn under the Consulate and the first Empire in France it is useful to have an idea of the regimental organisation. After the re-organisation of September 1803 when numbered line regiments once more came into being from the previous *demi brigades*, infantry regiments consisted of a number of fusilier companies, equivalent to battalion companies in the British army, and a number of grenadier companies. After September 1805 line regiments were augmented by the inclusion of light or *Voltigeur* company. The light infantry of the line also had grenadier companies, called *Carabiniers*, and light companies or *Voltigeurs*. In the infantry, shakos were tentatively introduced during the Consulate but supplies always lagged behind demand so that it was not until 1808 that the majority of regiments wore the shako. So short were supplies that Napoleon was forced to pillage the captured stores of the Prussians to provide shakos for his army.

The shako was bell-topped and bound around the top and lower edge in black leather with two reinforcing side stripes each side. At the juncture of the side stripes and the bottom band was a boss which held the brass chin scales. On the front of the shako was fitted a diamond-shaped plate bearing the regimental number. *Grenadiers* had in place of the black leather red lace, cords and plumes and the *Voltigeurs* had yellow shako ornaments. *Fusiliers* of the line had white cap lines above the universally worn national cockade of blue, red and white, above which was worn a plume or ball tuft. The *Fusiliers* wore a worsted tuft, differing in colour for each of the four companies: 1st, green; 2nd, sky-blue; 3rd, orange and 4th, violet. *Grenadiers* had a long, red plume and *Voltigeurs* had a yellow plume tipped with green or vice versa depending on the regiment. In the light infantry *Chasseurs*, equivalent to centre companies in the British army, had white cords to the shako and green plumes, *Voltigeurs* had green cords and a green-tipped yellow plume while the *Carabiniers* had a bearskin cap with red plume which was later abandoned for the shako with red plume. Light infantry plates were in white metal, as were the chin scales, and bore a crowned eagle over a French bugle horn.

In 1810 a new shako was approved and lines abolished although many regiments continued to wear them. Basically of similar shape and dimensions, the tuft previously worn by *Fusilier* companies was abandoned and a disc surrounded with woollen tufting bearing the company number substituted. Instead of the plume, *Grenadiers* retained their red ball and tuft when not in full dress. *Voltigeurs* also wore a ball and tuft in place of the long plume reserved for full dress. In 1812 new ornaments or shako plates were adopted, light infantry retaining the diamond shape but with a large bugle horn with the regimental number in the curl while line regiments adopted a semi-circular plate decorated with a row of wreaths and the regimental number in the centre. The whole was surmounted by the Imperial Eagle, with a grenade each side of the top

57

of the wreaths on the semi-circular portion. The non-commissioned officers of the infantry and light infantry were distinguished by differing shako cord colours, those of the line being threaded with gold wire and those of light infantry with silver wire. Officers on the whole preferred the cocked hat, perhaps in imitation of the Emperor, but their shakos usually had a band of gold lace around the top. This was sometimes omitted and a decoration of interlocking circles or a row of stars substituted which was in silver for light infantry officers. In full dress or '*grande tenue*' infantry officers wore white plumes tipped with red for *Grenadiers*, and green tips for *Voltigeurs*. Staff officers nearly always wore a cocked hat 'fore and aft' on the head with a rosette in the national colours as well as a plume coloured depending on whether they were attached to a brigade (blue-topped green) or division or Corps (blue-topped red).

Before leaving the Napoleonic era, another body of men must be considered: the Imperial Guard, almost an army within an army, with their own distinctions in dress and code of rules. Only two groups of infantry in the Imperial Guard wore the bearskin cap: the *Grenadier à Pied* and the *Chasseurs à Pied*. The former wore a brass plate, white corded cap lines and red plumes, while the latter wore a similar cap without plate and with a red over green plume. There was a red cloth patch to the back of the shako ornamented with a cross of white tape later changed to a white embroidered grenade. The other regiments of the Imperial Guard—*Fusilier Grenadiers, Flanquer Grenadiers, Fusilier Chasseurs, Flanquer Chasseurs, Tirailleur Grenadiers* and *Voltigeurs* together with the Pupils of the Guard—wore the shako, some with white tape 'V' side pieces and others the ordinary infantry pattern. There was also a variety of plume, cord and ball tuft colours.

The Peace of Paris and the restoration of the monarchy in France brought about minor changes to the army, the majority of which, like the civil service, continued to serve despite the titular change. The shako plate, of course, could not be tolerated and new supplies were quickly secured which bore the same semi-circular plate with regimental number but in place of the eagle was a crowned oval bearing the *fleurs de lys*. Napoleon's dramatic return from Elba and the ensuing '100 days' campaign had no effect on the shako or its plate except in the circumstances where a soldier had carefully kept his 'Imperial Eagle' plate and could hastily substitute it for the Bourbon insignia. The definite end of the Napoleonic era after Waterloo and the restoration of the Bourbons brought about the disbanding of the then French infantry, and in its place legions were formed in each of the departments. A new 'stove-pipe' shako was issued in 1815 with a royalist-styled plate and in 1820, when the numbered regiments were once more introduced, a new plate was sanctioned bearing the number and combination of the Bourbon *fleurs de lys*. 1825 heralded an entirely new shako with *Grenadiers* and *Voltigeurs* wearing a double pompon in red and yellow respectively. Light infantry had the added distinction of yellow lace around the shako. During the Bourbon period the red, white and blue cockade was naturally superseded by a white one.

Also, 1830 heralded another political upheaval in France with rivalries for the throne culminating in the succession of Louis-Philippe. Thus commenced the era of the 'cock' styled plate for the infantry. The immediate effect was that the tricolour cockade was restored with red on the outside and that double plumes were worn by élite companies. Another and perhaps more significant event occurred in 1830 which subsequently affected the head-dress and uniforms of the French and other armies who slavishly copied her fashions with amazing promptitude. This was the beginning of the long, French association with Algeria and North Africa. Although a new shako with upright sides was issued in 1837 it was the head-dress worn by the French troops in Algeria, the *Casquette d'Afrique* that was to be the future influence for the shakos of the French armies.

The *Casquette d'Afrique* was in red cloth with a blue band around the base and with a black leather peak. There were thin lines of blue down each side of the skull, the sides of which tapered towards the flat, slightly sunk-in crown. Ornamentation of the head-dress included the regimental number positioned above the blue band with the cockade in national colours above it. In the centre of the cockade, connected to the pompon by two strands or loops of blue, was a regimental ball button. A small button was fitted to the crown at the rear and connected to the back of the cap with another blue cord loop. Officers' versions were more lavish having gold lace bands around the shako at the top denoting rank and a design in gold cord of four loops in the centre of the top.

The immense popularity amongst the soldiers of the *casquette* made it the obvious choice on which to base the new shako introduced in 1844. At first regimental numbers alone were displayed but in 1845 a plate was issued. In marching order, inclement weather, etc, black covers were worn which bore the regimental number painted on the front.

In 1848 a revolution in France finally disposed of the monarchy and formed the Second Republic which lasted for three years before Napoleon proclaimed himself Emperor and set the seal on a Second Empire. The Royal Guard which had been created under Louis XVIII and continued by Louis-Philippe was transformed into a new Imperial Guard, copying and sometimes trying to outshine the original guard of the first emperor.

In 1856 a new lower shako was introduced trimmed in yellow for

59

infantry and bearing on the front a new eagle plate. The plate was introduced in 1852 and, for some reason, lacked a crown until 1855. In 1860 a further new pattern was introduced made of leather with the eagle plate. In 1884 the shako was finally abolished in the French army and the new lower *kepi* introduced in red cloth, similar to the original *Casquette d'Afrique*, with a blue cloth band and quartered with blue cord. The blue regimental number on a red square was worn in front, on the blue band above the black leather chin strap. Grey cloth or blue-grey cap covers were worn on active service while the kepi of the famed Foreign Legion was always worn with a white cover and neck flap.

In 1915 the helmet was introduced in France. Painted horizon blue to match the rest of the new uniform, it had a crest on the top and bore on the front a badge depending on the arm of the service of the wearer. The French had been experimenting with helmets since the early 1900s and had even introduced a metal skull cap to wear under the kepi.

The Imperial Guard dressed in their fur caps and shakos were swept away after 1870 and incorporated into the line. The association with Algeria and North Africa introduced into the French army a particular style of colonial troop which was to be widely copied by nations such as the United States who had no connection with the African continent. These troops dressed in their own particular fashion with a red cap; the *chechia* were the famed Zouaves.

(b) CAVALRY

The cavalry portion of the Imperial Guard created by Napoleon in July 1804 consisted of an assortment of cavalry including foreign troops such as Mamelukes, Polish Lancers and Tartars as well as a host of other bodies such as *Batallion des Marins de la Garde*, *Compagnie de Veterans de la Garde* and even the *Invalids de la Garde Imperiale*, a veritable army within an army in every sense.

The senior regiment, the Horse Grenadiers, like their foot counterparts wore the bearskin cap without a plate and fitted with a red plume on the left side. Officers' cap lines were in gold cord while those of the men were in a particular shape of orange termed *aurore*. The Imperial Guard *Gendarmes d'Élite* also wore a bearskin cap with white metal chin scales and a white grenade on a red cloth patch at the back. The dragoons of the Imperial Guard wore the brass, heavy cavalry pattern helmet with leopard-skin band extending over the peak, a black hair tuft on top of the metal crest and a flowing mane at the rear. A red plume was fitted in a holder on the left side. The *Chasseurs à cheval* of the Guard formed in 1804 wore a busby in blackish-brown fur with a red bag trimmed with gold cords and flounders which hung on the left side beneath a magnificent plume of green and red. The Lancers of the Guard incorporated in 1807 wore the lance cap or *czapska* with a crimson top piped in white for the 1st Regiment and scarlet piped in yellow for the 2nd Regiment. The plume was white for both regiments. The scouts or *Eclaireurs* comprised three regiments raised in 1813. The first wore a hussar-styled black shako; the second a tall cylindrical shako in crimson cloth with black leather peaks, the front one straight out and the back one capable of being folded down or up as required; the 3rd Regiment were dressed as lancers.

The heavy cavalry of the line wore a version of the typically French-style helmet introduced in 1762 but now with a peak and a brown fur turban. The crest was in brass as was the rest of the skull, topped on the front with a black hair tuft and ornamented along the top with a horse-hair mane which flowed to the rear. The peak was in black leather edged in brass and a red plume was fitted in the left side, except for one regiment who had white.

The senior cavalry regiments, the *Carabiniers*, wore bearskin caps up until 1809 when they were equipped with helmets and cuirasses. The helmet was of a special pattern not to be found in any other regiment; instead of an animal-skin band it had one in white metal bearing the initial 'N'. The horsehair mane so favoured was also omitted and a worsted comb in red fitted to the crest.

The *Cuirassiers* only received their helmets during 1802–4. This pattern had a steel skull and brass crest sporting a black tuft at the front above the typically French 'Medusa' head, and the ever-popular flowing mane along the top and down the back. The peak was in black leather bound around the edge in brass. A black fur turban encircled the helmet and a red plume was worn on the left side.

The hussars underwent a number of changes in head-dress. Forming part of the French light cavalry since the early eighteenth century, they had adopted the typical fur cap associated with their uniform but by the 1760s had taken to the mirliton. Élite companies and officers on occasion wore the fur busby, but even this distinction was withdrawn in 1812 when a shako similar to that worn by the *Chasseurs à cheval* was adopted. This had the distinction of red lace binding around the top and sides, and a red plume.

Around 1812 the tall cylindrical shako started to be adopted by the hussars; black for some regiments, red for others and light green for the 7th.

The *Chasseurs à cheval* had worn the helmet *à la Tarleton* until 1795 when they were ordered a shako but even so the helmet continued to be worn by some regiments as long as they were in good condition. 61

The result was that there was no uniform selection of head-dress for the twelve regiments.

The passing of the Empire did little to affect uniforms except to sweep away the eagles and crowned initial 'N'. The *Carabiniers*, reduced after Waterloo to a single regiment, continued to wear their previous pattern without the initial 'N'. In 1825 the strength of the regiment was augmented and five years later the Gallic cock badge of Louis-Philippe was the standard accepted military insignia.

Dragoons had received a new helmet which was distinctive in having a fur crest and no mane. In the early 1820s a complete departure from previous head-dress was introduced which was a brass helmet for dragoons and steel with brass trim for *cuirassiers*. The helmet had no animal-fur turban but instead a metal plate with grenade badge, a bristle-type comb along the top with a black hair tuft at the front and a flowing mane at the rear. Identification was by means of a worsted ball at the base of the red plume, each squadron having a distinctive colour. In 1840, however, dragoons made a return to the fashion of the early part of the century and adopted an animal-skin turban on their helmet, while the *Cuirassiers* adopted a black fur turban on their helmets with the added distinction of a red horsehair tuft on the front of the crest. Both these patterns continued in use during the Second Empire.

The lancers, converted from six dragoon regiments in 1811, continued to wear the brass helmet without a mane or tuft on the crest until the 1830s when Louis-Philippe introduced the *czapska* which owed little to the wide-sided styles of the Polish Lancers in Napoleon's employ. The leather skull was rather rounded, while the top was small and the waist extremely thin, almost reminiscent of the later German *Uhlan* head-dress which was also copied by the Belgians. With the reorganisation of the French cavalry into *Regiments de Marche* in 1870, the lancers with their distinctive head-dress disappeared for ever from the French army.

The *Chasseurs à cheval* continued to wear the shako until 1838 when they were ordered a busby of dyed curled lambswool with a boss in the front supporting a plume and with chin scales fitted each side. A red bag was worn on the left side for parades but dispensed with for active service.

Hussars had clung to their shakos which, although evolving in shape consistent with the other changes in head-dress of this style, were made in the colour of the cuffs of the dolman: 1st, 3rd, 5th, 6th and 7th being red; and the 2nd, 4th and 8th sky-blue. In 1860 hussar busbies of black curled lambswool were introduced but only, it seems, for parade wear as the shako continued to be worn for active service.

Turning briefly to the Imperial Guard of the Second Empire, we find the Guard Guides wearing a fur busby with black and white plume, the *Cuirassiers* a steel helmet without turban with black mane and the dragoons brass helmets with a horsehair mane. In addition were the badge, insignia and the crowned initial 'N'. Besides giving re-birth to an organisation which died in 1815, Napoleon III created rather than copied a completely new regiment: the *Cent-Garde*. Based loosely on the personal or Household Guard of the monarchs of France, the new regiment took precedence over every other French regiment including the Imperial Guard. The particularly rich helmet was in steel without a turban and with a brass plate bearing the crowned letter 'N'. The plume on the left side was red but the mane and front tuft were white. The regiment never at any one time consisted of more than eleven officers and 137 N.C.O.s and men, and in 1870 was incorporated into the line.

The French army's connection with Algeria and North Africa which gave the infantry the *zouaves*, contributed two formations to the cavalry: the *Chasseurs d'Afrique* and the *Spahis*. The former regiment was composed of both French and natives and wore the *czapska* in full dress but the *Casquette d'Afrique* in fighting dress. The lance cap, however, was retained only for a few years and disappeared in about 1846, the red casquette with its distinctive sky-blue band remaining the only head-dress. The *Spahis* were irregular cavalry recruited in Algeria; originally known as the *Spahis D'Alger*, *Spahis D'Oran* and *Spahis de Bone*, they were designated 1st, 2nd and 3rd in 1845. Native dress was worn but French officers wore a sky-blue kepi with gold lace.

After 1870 the shako and then the kepi became the preferred head-dress of the French cavalry except for the dragoons and *Cuirassiers* who received a new pattern of helmet with longer neck protection and lower skull. The *Cuirassiers* had the tuft on the front whereas the dragoons who now wore the same helmet did not have this detail. For active service, a muddy-brown cover was worn over the helmet and when the French cavalry took the field in 1914 they had their cuirasses and helmet covered in this way.

As with other countries like Britain with overseas territories, especially in the tropics, a cloth-covered cork helmet was issued and worn without ornament.

Prussia, German States and German Empire

(a) INFANTRY

The Prussian army had risen to a fine state of perfection under the guiding and dominating power of Frederick the Great but after his death in 1786 the stagnation which had started to set in during the later part of his life took another downward turn despite the efforts of Frederick William II. The infantry abandoned the tricorn hat and adopted the *casquet* which was a wide-brimmed hat turned up at the back and front with loops and buttons and with the royal monogram in brass on the front flap. The edge of the brim was bound in tape. Unlike the tricorn whose 'cock' was never allowed to be altered, the *casquet* was designed to allow the peaks to be folded down in bad weather. In 1798, when Frederick William III ascended the throne, the cocked hat was re-introduced for all line infantry except *Fusiliers* (a type of light infantryman in the Prussian army) who retained them until 1806.

Grenadiers who had worn the mitre cap with the metal front adopted a new pattern in 1798 which was given to grenadiers of line regiments the following year. The head-dress owed its major influence to the Russian pattern, but like the Austrian *casquet* introduced for infantry in 1770, it had a high false leather front. The crown and peak were in felt and the lower part of the crown was covered in a cloth flap in the regimental colour. The leather front was decorated with a grenade in brass above a brass plate bearing the Prussian eagle.

The uniforms and head-dress of some of the other German States did not differ to any great extent from Prussia whose rise to prominence in military power had made them worthy examples to be copied. Perhaps the one great exception was Hanover whose Elector, until the succession of Queen Victoria in 1837, was also King of England. In Baden, for example, grenadiers retained their metal-fronted caps, removing the tuft which was fitted to the top; while in Bavaria the infantry adopted a *casquet* with leather peak and skull, a comb holding a horsehair mane and a brass front plate with an oval with the State arms (see Plate 17). By the early 1800s the Bavarian infantry had been ordered a helmet based loosely on their previous pattern with certain similarities to the light dragoon 'Tarleton' and called a *raupe* (crested) helmet. The high leather skull was topped with a crest of bearskin for officers and worsted for the men, and the sides of the helmet fitted with yellow metal strips as reinforcement against sabre blows. Above the brass-bound peak was a metal band bearing the regimental title in the middle of which was fixed a crowned oval with the royal monogram. Grenadiers wore a red feather on the left side and Rifles one in green. The basic style of helmet adopted in the Bavarian army was also used, slightly adapted by Wurttemberg and Baden; the former with a leather crest topped with a worsted comb and the latter with a comb in metal and the fittings until 1807 in the colour of the buttons.

The crushing defeat inflicted on the Prussians at Jena in 1806 resulted in the final trappings of Prussian uniform and head-dress evolved over

10. 'Albert' pattern shako 1844–55

11. Officer's shako circa 1865 of the South Middlesex Rifle Volunteers

12. Officer's helmet 1878–81 of the Northants and Rutland Militia

13. Officer's shako of the Military Train circa 1855

14. Officer's metal dragoon-style helmet of the Yorkshire Dragoons

15. White 'Foreign service' helmet of the Royal Artillery

19.

2ᵉ Pionier-Abth. 2ᵉ 9ᵉ 14ᵉ 21ᵉ 34ᵉ Jnf.Regt. 2ᵉ Jäger Abth.

16. Print of the Prussian Infantry circa 1843 showing the newly adopted tunic and leather helmet

the previous eighty years being swept away. In 1809 the regular Prussian army, or what was left, was completely re-equipped and the model chosen by Frederick William III was his eastern neighbour, Russia. Shakos were officially introduced in 1807 for all except grenadiers who did not adopt them until 1810. The shako was of the bell-topped variety decorated with a band of lace around the top and bearing a metal plate on the front. Fusiliers and grenadiers wore a large exaggerated plume on the front fitted into a boss placed in the middle of the top band of lace.

In 1812 a shako verging on the French pattern was introduced; but in the following year, the new Russian pattern was adopted. This new pattern was distinguished by the concave top, the back and front rising leaving a dip in the centre. The Prussian shakos with their large plumes are well illustrated in the series of prints published in Berlin in 1815 executed by Wolf and Jugel (Plates 11 and 64).

The 1820s and 1830s were, for the infantry of most countries, the era of the shako. At first bell-topped, where there was little to distinguish one country from another in shape except for the badge, the shako later tended towards the French 'stovepipe' in some countries; although Austria, it seems, persisted alone in her own style with front and back peak and belling out only slightly. In 1840 the peaks disappeared and the sides became straight. Except for some minor modifications, the Austrians retained this shako until the latter years of the century.

Towards the end of the 1820s, the shako followed the pattern adopted by Russia; the height increased slightly, the bell became less pronounced and the exaggerated plume disappeared in favour of a much longer and thinner one. As with other patterns worn by Britain and Russia, the Prussian shako was decorated with white, worsted, plaited, cap lines that fitted each side at the top and hung down over the black leather peak. The Prussian eagle in brass was worn on the front beneath the corded boss holding the plume.

The Congress of Vienna in 1816 had reunited the various German States into a Confederation. The army of the Confederation comprised ten army corps of three Austrian, three Prussian and one Bavarian with the other smaller States forming the remaining three. This lasted until 1866 when the Federal army was dissolved.

Towards the end of the 1830s a general feeling towards uniform reform swept a number of countries, notably Russia who during this decade had dictated the military fashions throughout most of Europe. The French, as we have seen through their connections with Algeria and North Africa, managed to a certain extent to do away with the tight-fitting and constricting uniforms. While they were adopting a new, more comfortable pattern of shako, the Russians were 65 experimenting with a new styled helmet and tunic. Legend has it that Frederick William I V spotted one of these on the Russian Emperor's desk while on a visit and recognising its merit and advantage lost no time in introducing it into the Prussian army. The new helmet had a conical high leather crown with a back and front peak, the latter squared and edged in brass. The top of the helmet was ornamented with a brass cross, the branches pointing to the front, rear and each side. In the centre was fitted a spike for all regiments, which the artillery replaced with a ball in 1846. The back of the helmet had a brass strip running from the top ornament to the edge of the back peak. The front bore the Prussian eagle, differing between guard and line regiments, and chin scales were fitted each side with a cockade behind a fitment on the right.

The following year a horsehair plume was introduced for guards, grenadiers and certain line regiments for full-dress wear. The plume usually had a red band and was white for the guard and black for line regiments. The Russians introduced their spiked leather helmet in 1844 which differed in a number of ways from the Prussian model. In 1845 Sweden followed the Prussian lead and introduced a helmet based almost exactly on the Prussian pattern, but with a differing plate, which was retained by the infantry until 1854 when they switched suddenly to the French-styled shako.

The basic pattern of spiked helmet or *Pickelhaube* remained unchanged although minor modifications as to height, shape of peak, etc, were made from time to time. Modifications were carried out in 1857, 1860, 1871, 1887 and 1891, that of 1860 introducing a rounded front peak for all except generals, dragoons, Landwehr officers and the Prussian Palace Guard. Bavaria also retained the square-cut peak for those units wearing the *Pickelhaube* although, as was explained earlier, most infantry regiments wore the particularly Bavarian helmet with worsted crest up until the late years of the century. This helmet is immediately recognisable and bears a crown above the letter 'L' for Ludwig, King of Bavaria.

In 1854 *Jaeger* battalions abandoned the helmet for the shako made in leather. This shako was shaped to the head at the back and had a small rear peak as well as a larger one at the front. The plate was fitted to the front beneath a *feldzeichen* or oval-shaped cockade in the Prussian national colours. No cockade was worn behind the right chin-strap fastening. This pattern continued in use throughout the nineteenth century and survived the World Wars of the twentieth century as the German police helmet worn today. In 1871, when the German Empire was created, the shako had already been adopted by a number of *Jaeger* battalions of the member States, each with their differing plate and own *feldzeichen*.

The example set by Russia and Prussia in adopting the helmet was copied by a number of countries and in Britain the idea of adopting a leather helmet for the infantry was not only considered but had been tried experimentally by two regiments in 1853. It was, however, decided not to pursue the idea; presumably because of the outbreak of the Crimean War and the marked similarity between the Russian and British had the helmet been adopted. Stocks were relegated to British yeomanry regiments, many of which wore these leather helmets (Plate 6).

In 1871 the helmets of the general officers, all infantry except *Jaegers*, all dragoons, artillery and various other supporting arms of the new Imperial army were of the *Pickelhaube* type but with numerous differences in the metal of the trim and in the style and design of the plate. Prussian generals, for example, wore the eagle plate worn by the Guard regiments with the Guard star superimposed on the breast. The Guard eagle differed from the ordinary Prussian 'Line' eagle in having the wings flat out and straight at the top, the scroll carrying the almost universal motto of '*Mit Got für König und Vaterland*' with two curls, and having the eagle holding a sword and sceptre, whereas the 'Line' eagle held a sceptre and orb. Prussian general staff officers wore the same helmet with trim in silver while Bavarian, Mecklenburg, Hessian, Saxon and Wurttemberg generals and general officers wore the same helmet but with the helmet plate peculiar to their State. Most of the officers' helmets, especially those of higher rank, were beautifully gilded and often enamelled.

The scroll bearing the motto was not included on the eagle until 1860 and in later examples the word '*König*' has the addition of an 'e'. The scroll did not bear the word '*König*' for the 92nd, 5th, 153rd and 2nd and 3rd battalions of the 96th who substituted the word '*Fürst*'. Other regiments bore battle honours on the eagle plate, the 9th Grenadiers having 'Colberg 1807' with an oval above bearing an intertwined 'W.R.'; the 34th Fusilier Regiment had 'Peninsula and Waterloo' reminiscent of the battles fought allied to the British against Napoleon; while the 73rd Infantry bore the inscription 'La Belle Alliance'. The 'Line' eagle was adapted by a number of States by superimposing their own arms in the centre. These were Oldenburg, Anhalt, Saxon Duchies, Reuss, Schwarzburg and Mecklenburg, while Hesse, Wurttemberg, Bavaria and Saxony had their own particular plates. The special plates were also worn on the *Jaeger* shakos, but these were smaller in size.

The metal-fronted grenadier mitre cap was worn by three regiments: 1st Guard Regiment of Foot, Emperor Alexander's Guard Grenadiers and the Prussian Palace Guard Company. The first regiment had worn the metal-fronted cap bearing the Guard Star until 1894 when it was handed over to the Emperor Alexander's Guard Grenadiers and a new cap with an elaborate plate based closely on that used during the era of Frederick the Great was issued. The Prussian Palace Guard Company wore a cap similar to Emperor Alexander's Guard Grenadiers but with the front plate and flaming grenades, one each side to hold the chin scales and one at the rear, in silver.

The *Pickelhaube*, which lost the binding to the peak in 1887 when a leather chin strap was introduced (the binding was restored in 1891 and some regiments allowed chin scales), was not only distinguished by the badge on the front but also by the cockades fitted behind where the chin scales fitted to the head-dress. By this method not only could various States be distinguished but also the smaller areas of Prussia which all carried the same 'Line' eagle. The *land* cockade of the State or area was worn on the left and the Imperial cockade on the right. Bavaria, for example, had light blue and white; Prussia herself had black and white; Saxe-Weimar had green, black and yellow while the Hanse towns of Bremen, Hamburg and Lubeck had white and red.

(b) CAVALRY

The Prussian lancer cap of the period following Waterloo hardly changed for the rest of the century except that, as with the *Pickelhaube*, it became streamlined with the current trends and fashion. The early cap had a rounded leather skull with front and back peaks, above which was the traditional square top and belled-out top with a rather thinner waist than the contemporary British pattern. The eagle plate was fitted to the front left of the cloth-covered sides of the top, in similar fashion to the Russian cap, with an oval cockade in white with a black centre in the middle of the left side of the top. Lines encircled the waist of the cap and hung from the top right corner to the body of the wearer.

By 1867 the *czapska* was made entirely of black leather, similar to the British lancer officer's foul-weather cap, and a coloured cloth cover was provided to slip over the square top and sides for use on parades. Officers, as in the British army, usually supplied themselves with two caps: one without and one with the coloured sides to the top. The eagle plate was now placed on the front and other States copying the cap placed theirs, some in silver, others in brass, in the same place. The plume was white and the coloured cloth covers for the top were white, scarlet, light blue or crimson depending on the regiment. The 18th Uhlans (2nd Saxon) were alone in having dark red.

In typical hussar fashion, the Prussian hussars changed their head-dress with remarkable frequency adopting the mirliton or *flugelmutz*, the shako in various forms and returning towards the middle of the nineteenth century to the original hussar-styled head-dress: the busby.

Prints of the Prussian army of the 1840s (Plate 6) show the hussar with a tall cylindrical fur-covered busby with oval cockade in white and black at the top front holding a white plume, and a coloured bag falling to the left. By 1871 the busby had decreased considerably in height and was decorated with metal plates on the front. The oval cockade at the top was in the colours of the regiment's State of origin and the coloured bag, which was devoid of ornamentation, was in varying colours depending on the regiment. The 1st, 2nd and 17th Hussars wore the ancient 'death's head' badge; the first two with a metal ribbon with '*Mit Gott für König und Vaterland*' while the 17th had a gilt or brass ribbon beneath the silver 'death's head' inscribed '*Peninsula, Sicilien, Waterloo, Mars-la-Tour*'. Cap lines were fitted to the head-dress incorporated with a unique toggle. The bag was coloured white, scarlet, yellow, crimson, light blue, purple and dark red, the last two colours being for the 10th and 19th respectively. Brass chin scales were fitted to busbies of all ranks and all regiments.

The heavy cavalry had, like other countries, worn the bicorn cocked hat decorated with lace loops and a tall feather plume. In 1809 the *Cuirassiers* and *Garde du Corps* adopted an exact copy of the Russian helmet. The domed leather reinforced skull was surmounted by a leather comb, with the front edge and an inch of each side covered in brass, into which was fitted a black horsehair plume. The front and back peaks of black leather were edged in brass and chin scales were fitted each side. The large brass plate covering the front bore the Prussian eagle for *Cuirassiers*, and the star of the order of the Black Eagle or Guard star for the *Garde Cuirassiers* and *Garde du Corps*.

This pattern continued until 1843, when the radical changes in the Prussian army also affected the cavalry who now adopted a metal helmet. The helmet was similarly shaped to the leather infantry *Pickelhaube* except that it had a longer 'lobster tail' peak at the back to protect the neck. The body was in yellow metal for the *Garde du Corps*, *Garde Cuirassiers* and the *6th Cuirassiers* and in steel for all other *Cuirassier* regiments. The *Garde du Corps* and the *Garde Cuirassiers* wore the Guard star as their helmet plate while all *Cuirassiers* wore the Prussian eagle. In 1902 the *Royal Cuirassiers* (Grand Elector's Royal) changed to the so-called eagle of Frederick the Great with a scroll above inscribed '*Pro Gloria et Patria*', the eagle holding a sword and thunderbolts in its talons.

For parade purposes, the *Garde du Corps* and *Garde Cuirassiers* wore an eagle with spread wings in silver on the top of their helmet in place of the spike which was worn on other occasions. All *Cuirassiers* wore the spike.

The two Saxon heavy cavalry regiments also wore a yellow metal helmet with, as a plate, the arms of the State on a rayed star. In place of the spike worn by both regiments, the Saxon Guard Cavalry

(*Garde-Reiter-Regiment*) wore for parade purposes a silver lion with one paw raised resting on a shield bearing the crowned royal cypher.

The Bavarian heavy cavalry had, since 1815, been wearing a steel helmet with brass crest topped with a black fur comb but in 1875, *Cuirassiers* were converted to heavy cavalry where they adopted the Prussian pattern of spiked leather helmet with squared peak.

As with the leather *Pickelhaube*, the metal spiked helmet diminished in height towards the close of the century and the 'lobster tail' back became shorter. Another unit in the Imperial army wore a metal helmet, the *Jaeger zu Pferde* or mounted rifles. This helmet was in blackened steel not unlike the *Cuirassiers* in shape, with the plate and trim in silver. The plate was that worn on the dragoon helmets.

During the First World War, the *Pickelhaube* and other head-dress continued to be worn with canavas covers up until 1916 when the German steel helmet was introduced for all arms. Prior to this introduction a variety of helmets was issued in either thin pressed steel or field-grey felt. Usually the trim and plates were of a dull-grey metal.

The greatest single influence on head-dress in the immediate post-Napoleonic era was undoubtably that of Russia, who from 1803 introduced the shako throughout the infantry of her vast army. In 1805 the metal-fronted mitre caps were abolished for grenadiers, being worn only and up to 1914 by the Pavlovski Regiment. At first the shako was shaped on the French style with leather top, bands around the top and bottom and 'V' reinforcing pieces at the side; but in 1809 worsted plaited cap lines were added as were metal chin scales. A complete departure was made in 1812, when the shako was transformed into one of entirely Russian origin. The top had the back and front rising with a concave dip in the centre. The same ornamentation was worn but the plumes became longer and thinner.

In 1816 a new bell-top shako was introduced which was tall, slim and only slightly belled out at the top. The new shako bore a plate similar to that adopted for the British Waterloo shako (1812). This had the Imperial Russian crown over an indented oval plate and in the centre was the star of the Order of St Andrew. In 1828, however, the crowned double-headed eagle surmounting a French-styled semi-circular plate was adopted and continued in use on the spiked leather helmet adopted in 1844. Hussars and lancers who also wore this pattern of plate on their shakos and *czapskas* continued with it until 1855. The spiked helmet disappeared in 1855 except for the Preobrajenski regiment who wore it until 1881 by which time it had, like its Prussian and German counterpart, diminished in height and taken on a more rounded shape. The rest of the infantry adopted a French-styled shako which was also ordered for all other arms excepting lancers.

In 1881 an entirely new uniform and head-dress was ordered for the army. This resulted in a fur cap being adopted by the infantry which was anything but popular. In 1908 the fur cap was abolished and an undress peaked cap worn by the infantry; but the following year a lower version of the concaved-top shako of 1812 was ordered for guard regiments.

The Russian army fought in the First World War in their peaked caps and did not adopt a metal helmet for the troops until after the 1917 revolution when the Imperial Russian army disappeared. In the 1920s, when peace finally came to Russia, the French-pattern helmet was adopted with the Soviet hammer and sickle on the front.

After the Napoleonic wars the Swedish army, like many others, made a change in their head-dress and uniforms. The tall shako of the Russian style had the Swedish crown above the semi-circular French-shaped plate with, above that, a ribbon in metal. This fashion was copied directly from the Russians who allowed regiments that distinguished themselves in battle to add their scroll to illustrate their conduct. The 2nd Life Guards wore a large fur cap with metal plate at the front. The 1st Life Grenadiers wore a cap similar to the Prussian grenadier's cap worn between 1798 and 1809 but without ornamentation on the brass plate and without the grenade ball resting on top of the plate.

In direct imitation of Prussia and Russia, the Swedish infantry were ordered a leather spiked helmet in 1845 which was also ordered for the cavalry at the end of the same year. In 1854, however, the French influence which was now being felt almost everywhere persuaded the Swedish army to adopt the shako which was retained until 1909.

United States of America

The United States army had given up the tricorn hat in 1805 in favour of a felt shako which, in imitation of the British pattern, was cylindrical in shape; this was replaced around 1813 by a lacquered leather shako with a false front higher than the crown, again in direct imitation of the British shape, although the latter's shako was made of felt. The cap was decorated with a rosette on the top left side which held the plume, and plaited cap lines which ran from a button on the bottom left edge of the peak where it joined the shako diagonally across the front, to the top right opposite the plume and rosette. The plate was square with rounded indentations at each corner and seems to have born the eagle in an oval.

In the same year, the light and foot artillery and rifles adopted a bell-topped shako in lacquered leather. It was devoid of ornamentation in the form of lace but bore a rosette and button on the top front and an 71 eagle beneath with pierced out regimental number. Cap lines were fitted at the top of each side and hung down over the peak.

In 1820 the infantry gave up their shakos in favour of the bell top of 1813. In the Regulations of 1821 the distinguishing plumes are described as being five inches in length and yellow for artillery, white with a red top for light artillery, white for infantry, yellow for light infantry companies and green for rifles. The cap lines were gold cord and bullion for artillery and rifle companies' officers, the men wearing yellow and silver cord; and bullion for infantry officers and rifles, the men wearing white and green respectively.

The 1832 Regulations describe a shako similar to that worn in Britain and other European countries. The body was in black beaver six inches deep with a lacquered leather top eleven inches in diameter. The top was bound in leather and each side reinforced with 'V'-shaped leather straps. The plate and fittings were described as 'gilt eagle, number and scales . . .' It seems, however, that hardly had the regulation been published when a change of mind occurred and a new pattern was immediately ordered. The ordering of the British-styled bell top was probably due to the Head of the Clothing Board's report and dispatch of samples from Britain while on an official visit.

The new pattern as described in the 1833 Regulations was $7\frac{1}{2}$ inches high with a top the same measurement in diameter. The top was in leather as was the overlapping edge, bottom band and peak. The body was in black beaver. A leather chin strap was fitted to a brass button each side of the lower band. The ornaments included a 'gilt eagle and crossed cannons and number of the regiment as at present worn'. The infantry replaced the artillery crossed cannons with a stringed bugle horn. In the centre of the top was a grenade plume holder. The plume was white for infantry, red for artillery and light blue for the quarter-master sergeant and chief musician. The shako owes its shape to obvious French influences which were to prevail in American uniforms and head-dress from this date until the 1870s.

The shako of this pattern was also authorised in 1833 for the newly formed dragoon regiment, the United States army being singular in its lack of cavalry since the Revolutionary War. The helmet was to be the same as the infantry but

> . . . ornamented with a gilt star, silver eagle, and gold cord, the star to be worn in the front, with a drooping white horsehair pompon; the Field Officers to have a *small* strip of red hair, to show in front of their pompons.

The cap differed from that of the infantry in having a larger, broader peak as well as having corded cap lines fitted each side and attached to the body of the wearer. In 1845 both light and horse artillery were ordered to wear cap lines.

This pattern did not seem to enjoy much popularity with the soldiers and in 1844 a Uniform Board recommended several changes which were not, however, carried out. In 1850 General Orders No. 2 of the 13th February prescribed a new head-dress, the reason being that,

> . . . A large number of the Officers of the Army . . . have applied since the war with Mexico, to have a uniform less expensive . . . and better adapted to campaign and other service.

Once again the Regulations were suspended before being put into operation, and in 1851 General Orders of June prescribed a new shako based almost directly on the contemporary French pattern. The head-dress was to be in dark blue cloth and ornamented in various ways for the differing arms of the service. General officers had a lower band which rose to a point at the front in blue velvet with a gold embroidered wreath enclosing the letters 'U.S.' in silver; Engineers had a silver turreted castle; Ordnance had a shell and flame; Artillery, crossed cannons with the regimental number above; Infantry, a stringed bugle with the number in silver; Rifles, a trumpet with the regimental number and Dragoons, crossed sabres the edges uppermost with the number in the top quarter. Enlisted men were recognised not only by the emblem but by the colour of the cloth of the cap band: Artillery, scarlet; Infantry, light or Saxony blue; Riflemen, medium or emerald green and Dragoons, orange. Engineers had a blue band edged in yellow while the ordnance department had a blue band edged in crimson. For bad weather, a cap cover was issued which incorporated a neck flap which could be gathered and buttoned under the chin. The varieties of pompons ordered were staggering, each department having two-thirds buff and then in the colour allotted for the remaining portion: Adjutant General, white; Inspector General, scarlet; Quartermaster-General, Saxony blue; Subsistence, royal blue; Medical, emerald green; Pay, olive green; Engineers, black and Ordnance, crimson. The Infantry had Saxony blue; Artillery, scarlet; Rifles, emerald green; Dragoons, orange and A.D.Cs, all buff. For enlisted men, a yellow metal eagle was fitted to the base of the plume socket and the company number, except for engineers and ordnance, was placed at the apex of the coloured hat band.

In 1854 the coloured bands were abolished and a welt in the colour of the band was sewn to a plain blue band the same colour as the rest of the cap. In 1855 a campaign hat was ordered for the newly formed 1st and 2nd cavalry, and at the beginning of March 1858 the campaign hat was ordered for all arms of the service. Although in November a

73

new pattern forage cap with sloping top was ordered the 1851 shakos were handed out as forage caps to use up the store.

Both the hat and the forage cap were used by both sides during the American civil war. The hat was authorised to have three black ostrich feathers on the left side for officers and one feather for enlisted men. Cap cords which were gold or a mixture of gold and silk were to be worsted for the men, who also bore the corps insignia or the number of the regiment in brass on the front. On the forage cap the company number was displayed. The similarity between the forage cap and the French *kepi* can be clearly seen.

A new lower form of shako was introduced in 1872 for infantry and at the same time a blue felt helmet with spiked top was issued to the cavalry. The spike sported a horsehair plume and the cap was decorated with an eagle cap plate and caplines, cords and flounders. The cavalry wore yellow plumes and cap lines; the artillery, red and the signal corps, orange. The forage cap or *kepi* modelled on the French pattern was retained for undress wear. Blue felt helmets with white plumes were introduced for the infantry in 1881 to replace the shako. The felt helmet continued to be the full-dress head-dress of the American army up until 1902 when a radical change in uniform introduced a new pattern low-crowned cap, slightly belled out at the top. Khaki was introduced in 1902 and with it a buff-coloured campaign or field hat. At first the crown had only one dent in it but in 1912 four slight dents, similar to that later adopted by the Royal Canadian Mounted Police and the Boy Scouts and called by the Americans the 'Montana peak', were introduced.

This was the hat worn by the Americans when they entered the First World War in 1917 but it was soon replaced by the British-pattern steel helmet.

3: Accoutrements

Besides the head-dress and uniform there was a host of other items which went to make up the complete outfit of the fighting man, whether on foot or mounted. Some were of a practical nature such as sword belts, bayonet belts, ammunition pouches, water canteens and pouches while others were more of a decorative nature such as shabraques (saddle cloths), sabretaches, gorgets and sashes. Many items worn were also of a distinctive nature to enable a regiment or army to be recognised and friends distinguished from foe. These items included belt plates, head-dress plates, plumes, feathers, etc, many of them incorporated into the design of the head-dress, the usual place for such distinctive features, or in the uniform by the colour of the collar and cuffs, the number of bars of lace and their colour. Buttons were also used to bear regimental distinctions as was the cross-belt plate which fastened the belt holding the bayonet.

Rather than treat the various items under the headings of countries as was done in the previous chapters, it is felt that a better understanding and an easier method for identifying would result if the items were treated under their own headings. As most accoutrements of this nature bear either a recognisable symbol, the cypher of a monarch or head of state and in some cases the name of the regiment, attributing it to a country is not a serious problem, but the dating is. In following the evolution of the various items, it should not be too difficult to see where in the overall story the actual item under consideration fits.

(a) GORGET

The gorget was the final piece of the old full suit of armour worn by knights, and the half suits and other armour worn by pikemen, to survive the radical change brought about by the universal adoption of firearms in the world's armies. The gorget's or corselet's original function was to protect the throat of the wearer and as such it extended across the chest, up to the chin and downwards towards the chest. When it was finally discarded as a utilitarian object it was ordered to be worn in a smaller and bastardised form suspended on ribbons from the collar to denote a commissioned officer on duty.

A Royal Warrant of 1st September 1684 ordered that: For better distinction of our Officers serving Us in Our Companies of Foot, Our will and pleasure is, that all Captains of Foot wear no other corselet than of the colour of gold; all Lieutenants, black corselets studded with gold, and the Ensigns corselets of silver.

By the reign of Queen Anne this system had been abandoned and gorgets were ordered to be either gilt or silver, depending on the lace that adorned the officer's coat. The early patterns of the Marlborough wars were some seven inches across the top of the two ends and flat with the design raised from the back rather than being engraved. The usual motif incorporated was the royal coat of arms with the cypher divided each side of the crown.

By the time of the French Revolutionary wars the gorget had shrunk to a crescent-shaped object with the ends of the crescent almost touching. The usual design was the coat of arms, occasionally with the number of the regiment beneath, or the royal cypher crowned with either a scroll or the regimental number or title. On occasion the regimental badge, where entitled, was engraved.

The gorget was continued until 1830 in the British army although during the later years it tended to be discarded and during the Peninsular campaign when Wellesley (later the Duke of Wellington) was none too particular about uniform dress, it is doubtful whether it was even worn. A Lieutenant of the 88th Foot wrote that:

So long as we brought into the field well appointed with their sixty rounds of good ammunition, he (Wellesley) never looked to see whether their trousers were black blue or grey; and as for ourselves (the officers), we might be rigged out in all the colours of the rainbow if we favoured it. The consequence was that scarcely any two Officers were dressed alike . . .

Some of the earlier British gorgets had the design fixed to the crescent-shaped gorget but the majority had them impressed and later engraved. Regimental distinctions can often be found on them, but the use of the 'G.R.' cypher for the four Georges makes dating difficult.

In Prussia the style was also large and the design usually cast in gilt and mounted on the silver gorget which had the rim fitted with gilt beading. More often than not the design incorporated a trophy of arms and in the Prussian versions the central oval was usually enamel and bore the Prussian eagle. In France the gorget was used, as in Britain, to show commissioned rank but was soon put aside when epaulettes served as recognition for an officer. The French-pattern gorgets are easy to recognise as they retained the broad, half-moon shape with the ornament pinned on. In 1854 the gorget was still being worn by some officers of the French Imperial army.

Although generally discarded in most armies, the gorget was continued in use by the Swiss, Danish and other troops until the late nineteenth century. The Prussians kept it until the 1920s when the old comrades' associations used it. During the Nazi era in Germany the gorget found a new popularity amongst the standard bearers, old comrades' associations and the *feldgendarmerie* or military police.

Russian officers of the early nineteenth century wore the gorget, similar in shape to the pattern used by the British army, bearing the Imperial arms. Its function was to denote an officer on duty.

The gorget was usually fastened to two buttons on the collar by a ribbon, in Britain usually the same colour as the facings of the regiment. Although the gorget was abandoned in Britain in 1830, it is still remembered today in the red 'gorget patch' worn by staff and general officers. The Oxfordshire and Buckinghamshire Light Infantry before becoming a part of the Green Jackets also wore a 'gorget patch', the only regiment to do so, but with the added distinction of having it in white cloth.

(b) SABRETACHE

The origin of the 'sabretache' lies with the Hungarian hussars who wore an extremely tight-fitting uniform leaving no room for pockets. A pocket, or '*tasche*' in German, was slung from the sword belt and utilised in the same way as a purse. With the spread of the hussar style and mode of dress in the various European armies the sabretache was naturally copied. In Britain the sabretache seems first to have been worn by light dragoons in the 1790s, there being no hussars in the British army until 1805. The shape of the '*tasche*' was copied from the European style, but appears not to have been made of embroidered cloth but of leather covered in animal skin with the metal badge of the regiment placed in the centre of the large flap.

In 1805 four light dragoon regiments were converted to hussars and the opportunity taken to adopt the more elaborate embroidered sabretaches worn by the continental hussars. The 7th adopted a white cloth facing the sabretache; the 10th and 18th, blue and the 15th, red. In 1808 the 10th changed to red. The light dragoons, who by now had adopted the embroidered sabretache, had a dark blue cloth facing. The heavy cavalry had by 1812 also acquired a sabretache which differed in shape from that of the light cavalry by having the bottom edge rounded. It was faced in dark blue cloth.

The sabretache, whether for light or heavy cavalry, was edged all around with a wide band of lace, gold or silver depending on the lace of the regiment, and embroidered in the centre with the crown over the royal cypher. Permitted badges were also incorporated and in the early 1820s battle honours were added. By this period the sabretaches of the heavy cavalry were faced in the facing colour of the regiment and in velvet rather than cloth.

The rank and file wore black leather sabretaches, those of the light dragoons and hussars having a plain black flap; Life Guards, Royal Horse Guards and other regiments of dragoon and dragoon guards wore a black leather 'tasche' with a distinctive rounded bottom and the regimental badge on the flap. Lancers too, created in 1816, wore elaborate embroidered sabretaches until 1854. In that year embroidered sabretaches were abolished for all except hussars and light dragoons; officers and sergeants of the household cavalry, dragoons, dragoon guards and lancers were ordered a black leather sabretache with the flap bearing a regimental badge. Privates of the heavy cavalry had ceased wearing the black leather sabretache in 1831.

The hussars continued with the elaborate embroidered sabretaches until 1901, when this item of equipment was finally abolished. Certain other mounted officers wore sabretaches, these being staff officers who were distinguished by having the sabretache in red leather with the large flap adorned with the crown and royal cypher, and field officers of infantry and volunteers who wore the plain black leather *tasche* with perhaps a regimental badge, in the case of volunteers, fitted to the flap. Artillery officers also wore sabretaches: an elaborate embroidered version reserved for the horse artillery after 1855, and a black leather version used by the artillery in full dress and undress and which doubled as an undress sabretache for the horse artillery. The Royal Engineers also wore a black leather sabretache with a mounted gilt badge on the flap.

On the Continent the sabretache was usually kept exclusively for hussars, the originators of this piece of equipment. In France during the First Empire it usually bore the Imperial eagle with lace around the edge and minor working of leaves etc, the eagle forming the main part of the design. In Russia and Prussia the Imperial cypher was utilised as the basic design surrounded by elaborate embroidery, the more ornate denoting the higher rank of the wearer. In Austria too, the Imperial cypher was a favoured design while many of the Germanic states usually incorporated their state badge on the cloth-covered flap. A particularly handsome sabretache was that of the *Chasseurs à cheval de la Garde*, said to be the most expensively dressed regiment in Napoleon's army, which bore on its green cloth flap edged in gold lace an elaborate trophy of arms with the Imperial eagle in the centre. French *Chasseurs à cheval* favoured the French bugle horn badge on their sabretaches while the crossed cannon was the time-honoured badge of the artilleryman, except in Britain where only the Royal Marine Artillery utilised it on their embroidered sabretache.

In America the sabretache was not a favoured item of equipment and very few regiments wore them. The Boston Hussars who existed between 1810 and 1817 wore a green cloth-covered sabretache, the flap edged in gold lace with intricate working of russia braid around the edge and the initials 'B.H.' in the centre.

In the armies of the Honourable East India Company the sabretache was worn by light dragoon regiments up until the Indian Mutiny. After 1860, when many irregular cavalry regiments formed during the mutiny had acquired a more permanent existence, sabretaches were worn. Some of the Punjab light cavalry had brown leather *tasches*, edged in chain mail rather than lace with the regimental initial in the centre in metal. The Behar Light Horse for example had a brown leather *tasche* with the intertwined initials 'B.L.H.' The Governor-General's Body-guard continued to have the British officers wearing a sabretache in full dress with scarlet cloth flap edged in gold lace and elaborately embroidered up until 1947. The central design was the crown over the initials 'V.R.B.G.' and battle honours. Officers of the Madras Body-guard did not wear a sabretache, while that worn by the Bengal Body-guard had the flap covered in sky-blue cloth, edged in lace and bearing the crowned monogram 'B.B.G.' below a scroll inscribed 'BENGAL'. As officers of other Indian cavalry regiments wore the native dress the sabretache was not included.

(c) SHABRAQUES

This item of cavalry horse equipment was a development of the horse 'housings' worn during the seventeenth and early eighteenth centuries. In Britain, the Clothing Warrant of 1768 stated that:

> The Housings and Caps, except those of the Queen's, and Prince of Wales's Light Dragoons, to be laced with Gold or Silver Lace, and a stripe of Cloth in the Middle, of the Colour of that on the Men's. A Tassel to be on the Corners of the Housings, and One on the Middle of the Caps. To have Black or White Bear-skin to cover the Pistols. Those of the Queen's Light Dragoons to be of Leopard Skin, with Silver Fringe; and those of the Prince of Wales's to be Black Cloth, with Stripes of Goat-skin and Silver Lace.

The Housings and Caps of other ranks and officers were in the facing colour of the regiment except in the King's Dragoon Guards, Royal Dragoons, 7th Dragoon Guards and the King's, Queen's and Prince of Wales's Light Dragoons. The first two had red, the 7th buff, the King's 79 and Queen's Light Dragoons white, while those of the Prince of Wales's Light Dragoons were black with 'stripes of White Goat-skin'. The rank of the regiment was embroidered on the housings on a red ground with a wreath of roses and thistles or 'particular Badge of the Regiment; as on the Second Guidon or Standard'. The royal cypher with crown above was displayed on the holster caps with the regimental number beneath.

By the beginning of the nineteenth century, the use of housings and holster covers had been abandoned except by mounted cavalry drummers, who wore the housing only, and general officers who still wore the holster covers embroidered with their badge of rank. In their place the cavalry adopted the shabraque, a cloth which covered the saddle, extended to the rear and also forward covering the holsters, wallets, etc. As with the housings, each regiment retained its individuality by displaying on the particular coloured cloth various ornaments in gold, silver and silk embroidery. The Dress Regulations of 1846 give the following details concerning shabraques:

> 1st LIFE GUARDS—blue cloth, with pointed ends; laced round with two and a half inch gold oak-leaf pattern lace, which has a red silk stripe worked in its outer edge: *Embroidery*—on the hind-corners, a garter star proper, above which is a double cypher, L.G., surmounted by a scroll, bearing the words, 'Peninsula, Waterloo,' and a gold crown above all. On the front corners, the double cypher L.G., surmounted by a small figure '1', and a gold crown above all. *Seat Cover*—black lambskin.

The 2nd Life Guards had blue cloth with round corners, with the lace mounted on a scarlet cloth ground. The decoration on the rear consisted of the garter star with '2' beneath, 'Peninsula' to the left and 'Waterloo' to the right. Above it all was the Queen's crest. The front ornamentation was similar but it omitted the number '2'. The Royal Horse Guards had a scarlet shabraque edged with two rows of gold lace showing blue cloth between, the corners embroidered with a crown and star and the honours 'Waterloo' and 'Peninsula'.

The shabraque for the dragoons and dragoon guards was stated in the same regulations as:

> Dress Shabraque of blue cloth; square corners, embroidered with regimental device, and trimmed with gold lace. Double border of gold lace for Dragoon Guards, of the same pattern as for the trousers, the outer row an inch and three quarters, the inner one inch wide. The Officers of Dragoon Regiments have one row of lace only, two and half inches wide.

17. *Private McGuire of the 33rd Regiment being captured by Russian soldiers in the Crimea. This plate shows the uniforms, head-dress and equipment of the opposing armies*

18. *Officer's lance cap of the 21st Empress of India's Lancers* circa *1900*

The light dragoons had a blue cloth shabraque,

> . . . the fore part round . . . embroidered with the cypher V.R. in gold,
> and a crown; the hind part . . . with rounded corners embroidered
> as the fore part, but larger, and with the addition of the badge and
> motto of the regiment; trimmed with two inch gold regulation
> lace . . .

Lancers also wore the same description of shabraque as the light dragoons
but hussars were ordered one of blue cloth for the 7th and 8th, scarlet
for the 10th and 15th and crimson for the 11th, the 'cherry pickers'. It
was to be trimmed with 2½-inch gold lace, striped with blue and to bear
the royal cypher and crown on 'the fore part of a diagonal shape'. The
hind part was pointed and embroidered with the royal cypher, crown
and regimental devices, usually an elaboration or enlargement of that
borne on the sabretache. In the 7th, 8th and 10th the seat cover was in
leopard skin while in the 11th it was in black lambskin. The undress
shabraques of the hussars were also particularly attractive being leopard
or 'spotted tiger-skin' in the 7th, 10th and 15th; black lambskin edged
in scarlet for the 8th but vandyked crimson for the 11th. The 15th also
had a blue cloth undress shabraque trimmed with red cloth vandyked.

Mounted infantry officers wore a saddle cloth rather than shabraque
in the facing colour of the regiment edged in gold lace and scarlet.
The holsters were to be covered in black bearskin, except for tropical
climes where black patent leather was ordered.

The Royal Horse Artillery officers and officers of the field batteries
and battalions had a blue cloth shabraque with rounded corners bearing
on the rear the field gun and motto 'Ubique'. It was edged in a wide
band of gold lace and in scarlet cloth welt.

By the end of the nineteenth century the shabraque appears to have
fallen into disuse in a number of dragoon and dragoon guard regiments,
the Dress Regulations of 1894 stating that they were to be of authorised
regimental pattern for regiments retaining them but 'must not be re-
introduced in regiments which have discontinued or may discontinue
its use . . .' The above also applied to the hussars and lancers. In the Dress
Regulations of 1900 the shabraque was abolished for all except the
household troops. Lambskin was introduced for the dragoons and
dragoon guards, lambskin or leopard for the hussars, the 15th being
allowed to embroider theirs with crossed flags, and lambskin for the
lancers.

With the abolition of full dress and the final onslaught of modern
armoured vehicles the lamb- or leopard-skin shabraque disappeared,
except for the household troops, with the cavalry troop horse.

Light dragoons of the armies of the East India Company also used the   81 shabraque, shaped and adorned similarly to that of their British counter-parts. The colour of the shabraque of the Madras Light Cavalry is particularly striking being a French grey adorned in silver lace and with silver embroidery.

In the United States, saddle cloths worn at the time of the American Civil War are described in the Regulations of 1864. General officers were ordered 'housings' or shabraques as we know them which covered the saddle and holsters or wallets. These were described as:

> . . . of dark blue cloth, trimmed with two rows of gold lace, the outer row one inch and five-eighths wide, the inner row two inches and one fourth; to be made full so as to cover the horse's haunches and forehands, and to bear on each flank corner the following ornaments, distinctive of rank, to wit: for the *Major-General Commanding the Army*—a gold-embroidered spread eagle and three stars; for other *Major-Generals*—a gold-embroidered eagle and two stars; for a *Brigadier-General*—a gold-embroidered eagle and one star.

General staff officers wore a saddle cloth only of 'sufficient length to cover the saddle and holsters' in blue cloth edged with a single band of gold lace.

For the mounted service a saddle blanket was supplied '. . . close woven of stout yarn of an indigo blue colour, with an orange border 3 inches wide, 3 inches from the edge . . .' In the centre of the blanket in letters '6 inches high, of orange colour' were the letters 'U.S.'

Field and regimental staff officers wore a saddle cloth which did not cover the holsters but was in blue cloth and of similar shape to that described above.

Again, with the demise of the use of horses in the cavalry, the saddle cloth disappeared for ever. In the war with Cuba and Mexico in the early years of the twentieth century and the First World War the saddle cloth was not worn on active service, being merely an item of full-dress horse equipment of no functional use in modern warfare.

On the Continent, the shapes of the shabraques followed the unwritten rules by which British shabraques were shaped. These were squared for heavy cavalry and pointed, in some cases to the point of absurd exaggera-tion, for the dashing light cavalry and hussars. In France the heavy cavalry, dragoons and *Cuirassiers* differed in that they clung to the housing, which covered the rear, and wore a lambskin seat cover which extended forward over the holsters and wallets. The *Chasseurs à cheval* in *grande tenue*, equivalent to the British review order, wore a leopard-skin shabraque edged in lace, with a scarlet welt and green cloth; while in fighting dress they had a green shabraque with embroidered motif on the pointed rear end. The *Cuirassiers* had squared housings edged in white or silver lace and bearing an embroidered grenade in the rear corner. Officers usually had cloth holster covers with distinctive double pointed flaps in place of the lambskin. The regimental number was borne on the distinctive square-sectioned valise worn at the rear of the saddle. For hussars and light cavalry this was a round-sectioned valise.

French lancer regiments of the guard had a blue pointed cloth shabraque decorated on the edge with a line of crimson piping, white piping, a band of crimson and another line of white piping. The pointed rear was decorated with an embroidered eagle and the front portion covering the cloak bore the crowned initial 'N'. Other lancer regiments wore the pointed shabraque in a variety of colours, red usually denoting a trumpeter.

In the Russian army of the post-Waterloo period the housings and holster covers were retained by various heavy cavalry and guard regiments. Amongst them was the Regiment of Horse Guards who wore a blue cloth edged in red cloth on which was superimposed two bands of gold lace. The same edging applied to the holster covers. The ornamentation was the Guard star in the rear corner of the housing and on the holster covers. The *Life Guard Cuirassier* Regiment wore a light blue housing and holster covers to match the facing colour of their white full dress coatee, edged in two bands of silver lace and once more bearing the Guard star.

Lancers and dragoons wore a shabraque with rounded front and rear, the former in blue edged with a scarlet band with two bands of gold lace for the Guard Lancers and bearing on the rear part only the crowned Imperial monogram. For officers this was worked in gold but for other ranks in red worsted. In the dragoons the shabraque was in green cloth and of the same design, the Life Guard Dragoon Regiment having the scarlet edging with gold lace bands and embroidered Imperial cypher on the rear. Hussars differed in that, in common with the majority of other hussars of various countries possessing them, they had a pointed rear shabraque. For the Guard Hussar Regiment this was in blue with the edge elaborately decorated in yellow lace with vandyked inner edge, piped in scarlet and then elaborately worked with a tracing of braid, forming loops at the points. The Imperial crowned monogram was displayed on the hind quarter.

The Prussian army of about 1810 also used the housings and holster covers in the *Garde du Corps*. These were red with an edging of two bands of white lace with a light blue between. The small holster flaps (not covers) were pointed and edged in the same manner and bore, as did the rear part, a crown over the Guard star. Officers wore the same but with a silver embroidered crown over the Guard star. The Guard artillery and other artillery units favoured a blue cloth shabraque edged   83 with a band of black material and piped in red. In the case of the Guard, the Guard star was featured on the rounded portion of the hind part.

Cuirassiers wore a housing with holster covers in their facing colour edged with a broad band of white or silver lace. Plate 114 shows a selection of Prussian horse furniture of the 1890s; the *Garde du Corps, Garde Cuirassiers* and *Cuirassiers* will be noticed to be still wearing the housing with matching holster or wallet covers, although for parade wear *Garde du Corps* officers wore a complete saddle cloth with additional holster covers.

(d) CROSS-BELT PLATES, WAISTBELT PLATES AND BUTTONS

Besides the distinction afforded by the colour of the facings of a regiment, additional individuality was accomplished by various items of strictly regimental pattern. The cross-belt plate which held the sword or bayonet belt together seems to have been sanctioned in the British army some time in the 1750–60 period when the waistbelt, which had held the sword or bayonet, was slung over the shoulder for added convenience.

The waistbelt had been fastened usually with a plain brass buckle but after the belt was worn over the shoulder this was superseded by an oval plate which bore the regimental number commonly with the addition of the crown and a spray of laurels. The clothing warrant of 1768 stated that regiments of horse and light dragoons were to wear the sword belt over the right shoulder and twenty years later dragoons and dragoon guards were ordered to wear the sword belt in the same manner.

The colour of the metal for cross-belt plates of infantry and cavalry usually depended on the colour of the lace that adorned the officers' coats, gilt for those wearing gold lace and silver for those wearing silver lace. There were, however, as with all regulations and rules governing dress, exceptions. The oval plate started to lose favour during the first decade of the nineteenth century and by the middle of the reign of George IV seems to have completely disappeared. In its place was an oblong or rectangular plate which for officers was usually lavishly embellished with the regimental number, titles (county titles were awarded to the majority of regiments in 1782) and a profusion of battle honours. Regiments which were authorised a special badge also bore this prominently on their plates.

In 1830 the distinction of colour for lace was abolished and the regular army ordered to adopt gold lace, silver being retained for the militia and volunteers. This does not mean that officers' plates were all gilt. The rectangular back-plate was usually gilt, either highly polished or frosted, and the various designs, numbers and distinctions were often made in silver and fitted on. In 1855 the cross-belt was abolished for infantry officers and other ranks were issued with new, improved equipment in the 1850s. The elaborate cross-belt plate disappeared for all except Highland regiments who retain them to this day, slinging their swords from cross-belts and not waistbelts.

The cavalry by the time of the issue of new uniforms during the latter years of the Napoleonic wars had abandoned the cross-belt and adopted a waistbelt. The hussars on their formation in 1805 had adopted a waistbelt which was secured with an elaborately worked snake fastening. The heavy cavalry adopted a rectangular gilt plate on which was displayed the crown over the royal cypher. This pattern with differences in the background and change of cypher continued in use with cavalry officers until the demise of full dress.

In 1855 officers were ordered a waistbelt which usually bore the regimental number in the centre surmounted by a crown with the regimental title in a circle around the outer edge. Other ranks also wore regimental pattern clasps until the introduction of the 'Universal' locket which bore the royal crest in the centre and the garter motto, *Honi soit qui mal y pense*, in a circle around the outer edge.

Cavalry troopers adopted a snake fastening for the light cavalry and a rectangular plate with regimental distinctions for the heavy cavalry. Towards the end of the century all troopers were issued with a belt bearing a snake fastening.

Until 1767 buttons in the British army bore no set design; in fact many were plain and only officers, if they cared to, had buttons with some non-military motif on them. In 1767 it was decided that in future buttons would bear regimental numbers.

WAR OFFICE

21st September 1767.

SIR,

His Majesty having been pleased to direct that the Number of each Regiment of Dragoon Guards, Dragoons and Foot (including the Regiment of Invalids), shall be respectively mark'd on the Buttons, at the next cloathing, as likewise on the uniforms of the Officers, when they shall make new ones . . .

Two months later permission was granted to the three regiments of dragoon guards to have initials rather than numbers on their buttons. The colour of buttons for officers once again conformed to the colour of lace worn on the coat. Other ranks of infantry wore pewter which they retained up until the introduction of the tunic in 1855. In the 85 cavalry other ranks' buttons were either white metal, pewter, yellow metal, bronze or brass.

After 1855 all other ranks' buttons were brass and those of the officers gilt, militia having silver and white metal and volunteers silver or, in the cases of rifle volunteers, bronze or black depending on the style of their uniforms. In 1871 regimental pattern buttons were discontinued for the rank and file of the British army, except for Corps, and a general service pattern button in brass displaying the Royal Coat of Arms was adopted. This pattern continued for other ranks until 1924 when regimental buttons were once again sanctioned.

Officers continued to wear the numbered buttons until 1881 when the new territorial system introduced under the Cardwell reforms linked numbered battalions into regiments known by territorial or other titles. The new badges were adapted for use on the buttons. The introduction of service dress in 1904 brought with it, for officers, bronze versions of the full dress gilt buttons; other ranks retained the brass general service button introduced in 1871.

In 1803, numbered regiments in the French army underwent a reformation when the Consular Order of 28th September created regiments in place of the demi-brigades formed since the abolition of the Royalist army in August 1793. Each numbered line regiment bore the number on its buttons within a French scroll, which was often used on British buttons. The buttons were hollow-backed in brass. Engineers, artillery, etc, instead of numbers bore the symbol of their corps, the helmet and breastplate of the engineers and the crossed cannons of the artillery. The *Cuirassiers* bore the grenade on their buttons, the same as used on their other appointments. On its formation in 1831 the Foreign Legion adopted a brass button with, in a circle on the outer rim, the words *Legion Étrangere*.

In the States that formed the German Empire numbered buttons were worn by the regiments. However, the number did not denote the rank of the regiment but the company, battery or squadron of the wearer. Various regiments, especially those of the Guard, wore a button with a germanic letter 'L' or crowned letter 'L'. The *Leib-Kompagnien* of the 1st Guard Regiment of Fusiliers, the *Garde du Corps* and the *Leib Guard Hussar* Regiment among others bore the letter 'L' while the crowned 'L' was used by the *Leib-Kompagnien* of the 115th Infantry and the 25th Dragoons.

Other buttons bearing state insignia were worn by general officers and staff officers, as well as non-commissioned officers, on the collars of the full dress tunics. There were seven different designs, each bearing the motif of the wearer's state, which were used to denote rank between the various grades of non-commissioned officers.

In the United States of America buttons were numbered after the British fashion, the Massachusetts Provincial Congress ordering, in July 1775, that the buttons of the state regiments should be numbered and made of pewter. There were also a number of other styles and types worn by volunteer and militia units, occasionally bearing their title.

By 1864 the types of buttons in use had been strictly regulated unlike the British army where regimental patterns abounded. General officers and officers of the general staff had a gilt button with spread eagle while engineers had a button bearing the eagle holding a scroll in its beak inscribed *Essayons*, 'a bastion with embrasures in the distance surrounded by water, with a rising sun'. The Corps of Topographical Engineers had a button bearing the shield of the United States on the top half and the letters 'T.E.' in Old English on the bottom. The Ordnance had the crossed cannons and grenade or bombshell with a circular scroll across the top bearing the words 'Ordnance Corps'. For officers of artillery, infantry and cavalry the button sanctioned bore:

> . . . a spread eagle, with the letter A, for artillery—I, for Infantry—C, for Cavalry, on a shield . . .

Other ranks of all arms wore a yellow metal button the same as in use by the artillery, etc, but omitting the letter on the shield.

Neither French nor Prussians were advocates of the cross-belt plate, preferring in its place either a continuous cross-belt adjustable where it held the bayonet frog or pouch, or with a plain brass buckle. In the United States the cross-belt was, at the time of the Civil War, in black leather and the plate in brass bearing the letter 'U.S.' The Confederate States adopted a similar plate marked 'C.S.A.' There was never any individual regimental identification.

The rectangular sword-belt plate ordered for all officers and enlisted men in 1864 bore:

> . . . a silver wreath of laurel encircling the 'Arms of the United States', eagle, shield, scroll, edge of cloud and rays bright. The motto, 'E PLURIBUS UNUM' in silver letters, upon the scroll; stars also of silver according to pattern.

Waistbelt plates or clasps were universally adopted during the latter years of the nineteenth century. Many were rectangular in shape, some were plain such as those of the French infantry while others bore either pinned-on designs or designs stamped into the metal. The unified German Empire had as a universal plate one bearing a double circle between which was inscribed *Gott mit uns* with, in the centre, the Imperial crown. This plate was in dull grey metal.

In France rectangular plates with pinned-on designs were popular in 87 cavalry regiments, and the *Gendarmerie* and the personal household troops of the King and the two emperors wore elaborate plates bearing the royal or Imperial arms with their titles incorporated in scrolls.

Other countries such as Russia also adopted the rectangular style of plate with a design fitted to it. In Britain, as has already been explained, the cross-belt plate gave way to the waistbelt clasp. This can be found in many variations for regular, militia and volunteers, as it was universally adopted except for the artillery, engineers, cavalry and Highland regiments. In 1904 dress regulations ordered a waist sash to be worn by infantry officers in place of the waistbelt. The clasp finally disappeared for officers although it was still retained by infantry regiments on the white belt of the Slade-Wallace equipment used for full dress wear and walking out, and by the Guards, who to this day retain an individual regimental pattern locket.

(e) EPAULETTE

Epaulettes developed from the bunches of ribbons worn on the shoulders and knotted to prevent the cross-belt from slipping. These knots developed into shoulder straps in some armies and it was only a matter of material and decoration that turned it into the epaulette towards the end of the eighteenth century.

In the British army, infantry officers were ordered in the Clothing Warrant of 1768 to wear epaulettes,

> The Officers of Grenadiers to wear an Epaulette on each Shoulder. Those of the Battalion to wear One on the right Shoulder. They are to be either of Embroidery or Lace, with Gold or Silver fringe.

Cavalry officers were also ordered epaulettes in the same warrant but only on the left shoulder. Other ranks of the cavalry were ordered an epaulette in the facing colour with narrow yellow or white tape around it and with a worsted fringe. Again, this was worn only on the left shoulder.

An order of December 1791 stated that:

> Two Epaulettes are to be worn upon the General Officers Frock Uniform, in the manner as they are now worn on the Great Uniform; and the *Effective* Field Officers of all Regiments (Cavalry as well as Infantry) shall likewise be distinguished by wearing an Epaulette on each shoulder. Grenadier Officers, who now wear two Epaulettes are to have the Addition of a *Grenade* Embroidered on each—and the Light Infantry Officers that of a *Bugle-Horn*.

The infantry private wore epaulettes on the new pattern short jacket introduced in the 1790s with a worsted fringed tuft for battalion companies and rounded worsted wings for the flank companies. These continued in use until 1855 when the introduction of the tunic re-introduced the shoulder strap. Officers' epaulettes, which during the first half of the nineteenth century had become elaborate examples of the laceman's art, also disappeared in 1855.

Other cavalry ranks had since the early part of the nineteenth century worn shoulder scales. These came in a variety of forms and shapes. The early type, especially popular with the volunteer yeomanry cavalry, were in the form of wings decorated or reinforced against sword cuts with a row of interlinking rings. The other style which came into general use after Waterloo was the solid metal crescent and scale shoulder strap. These were worn by heavy cavalry, light dragoons and lancers; hussars alone spurning this shoulder protection. The yeomanry cavalry also adopted this general style and a great variety can be found. The 17th Lancers had the metal crescents decorated with a skull and crossed bones superimposed on crossed lances. In 1855 when the tunic was introduced the metal scales were abandoned. There was some later use of this type of scale, usually decorated with rows of interlinked chains, by some yeomanry cavalry regiments.

A revival of epaulettes occurred during and after the Indian Mutiny when cavalrymen adorned their shoulders with curb chains to ward off sword blows. These were enlarged and developed and the 'chainmail' type of shoulder epaulette is still worn today in full dress by cavalry regiments and others.

The Royal Navy, as did the majority of other navies, clung to the epaulette until the decease of full dress. The strap bore the officers' rank and a silver anchor was placed inside the crescent.

A particularly attractive form of epaulette was that worn by flank company officers. These 'wings' were as follows:

> . . . the straps having three rows of chain, and gilt centre plate, bearing a bugle in silver; a row of bullion one inch and a quarter deep at the centre, diminished gradually towards the point . . .

In grenadier companies the gilt plate bore a silver grenade, with a bugle for light infantry regiments. These patterns disappeared in 1855.

The Imperial line infantry of Napoleon decorated their blue uniform coats with red worsted epaulettes and fringes, while the light infantry centre companies wore epaulettes without fringes. *Carabiniers* and *Voltigeurs*, the grenadier and light companies of the light infantry, wore fringed epaulettes in red, yellow and green.

In 1812, when the short jacket or *habit-veste* was introduced, the 89 epaulettes were replaced by shoulder straps piped red for grenadiers and yellow for *Voltigeurs*. Officers still continued to wear epaulettes as a badge of rank, captains and lieutenants wearing an epaulette on the left shoulder only.

The introduction, or re-introduction, of numbered regiments in 1820 was also a convenient time to introduce a new uniform. Red epaulettes indicated *Grenadiers*, with yellow for *Voltigeurs*. Both had fringes while centre companies wore epaulettes without fringes. The *Chasseurs d'Orleans*, in 1848 re-titled the *Chasseurs à pied*, wore green fringed epaulettes; those of the rest of the infantry remained unchanged until 1860. In that year another drastic change in the design of the infantry-man's uniform meant the ordering of red and yellow fringed epaulettes for the *Grenadiers* and *Voltigeurs* respectively and the introduction of green fringed epaulettes piped in scarlet for centre companies. The distinctive flank company epaulettes continued up until January 1868 when this distinction was abolished and all line infantry wore the green epaulettes piped in scarlet.

The French heavy cavalry always wore red worsted fringed epaulettes while the lancers formed in 1811 did not immediately adopt the lancer uniform and white epaulettes, which was to be their distinctive colour until lancers were abolished in 1870. *Chasseurs à cheval* wore red worsted fringed epaulettes until they adopted a frogged hussar-style jacket with-out epaulettes in 1848. The *Chasseurs d'Afrique* formed in 1831 were by 1840 wearing a single-breasted long tunic with lance cap and, unusual in the French army at this time, brass shoulder scales. In 1863 the tunic and scales were replaced by a hussar-styled dolman with no epaulettes. After the re-organisation and rationalisation undertaken after the defeat of the French army in the Franco–Prussian War of 1870 only the heavy cavalry continued to wear the fringed red worsted epaulettes.

In the Imperial Guard of Napoleon I, the *Grenadiers* wore scarlet fringed epaulettes while the Guard *Chasseurs à pied* wore epaulettes with green straps and scarlet fringes. The Horse Grenadiers had no fringes on the troopers' epaulettes while the fringeless epaulettes of the Guard Dragoons were in orange. In the Guard, lancers' epaulettes were white with white fringes except for the 2nd Regiment, known as the 'Red Lancers' because of their distinctive red jackets, who wore yellow epaulettes. The two regiments of *Cuirassiers* added to the Guard on the restoration of the Bourbons in 1816 wore white epaulettes. After 1822 the Royal Guard infantry also wore white epaulettes. The founding of the Second Empire brought back to the Imperial Guard the *Grenadiers* with their distinctive red epaulettes and introduced for the *Garde Voltigeurs* red epaulettes with the shoulder strap piped in yellow. The *Cent-Gardes*, the bodyguard created by Napoleon III, had unusual scarlet epaulettes fringed in gold while the *Garde Cuirassiers* and dragoons wore white fringed epaulettes.

The collapse of the Empire in 1870 and the definite establishing of the Republic saw the end of bodyguard troops and in their place was created the *Garde Republicaine* which had, and still has, foot and mounted troops.

In the Prussian army shoulder straps were far more popular than metal or lace epaulettes in the post-Waterloo period. When they were introduced they retained their distinctive design until abolished in 1866. Under the new Imperial régime, they were re-introduced by William II and continued to be worn in full dress until the First World War. For the junior officer ranks the epaulette was unfringed. Fringes were used for ranks above major, becoming thicker towards the most senior ranks of general and *General-Feldmarschall*. The Prussian epaulettes, like those of the Russian army, were distinguishable by the nearly round end and short shoulder strap. The rounded part decorated with a metal crescent in the Prussian army did not figure on Russian epaulettes where, like those of the British Royal Navy, the crescents were formed in gold wire and bullion.

The strap and inside portion of the rounded end were in cloth of the facing colour of the regiment with the edge of the strap decorated in lace or silver with a coloured double line depending on the wearer's state. The top of the strap was ornamented with a button and, just before the crescent, a silver lace bar representing the strap on the coat, by which the epaulette was held in position. The regimental number appeared inside the epaulette crescent; on its own for lieutenants, with one 'pip' beneath for *Oberleutnant*, and one 'pip' each side for *Hauptmann Rittmeister*. This ranking process was repeated with the fringed epaulettes which commenced with the rank of major, and ended with *Oberst* with the 'pip' each side of the regimental number. The more heavily fringed epaulette of a *Generalmajor* had no metal decoration within the crescent at all. The next rank up, the *Generalleutnant*, started the 'pip' sequence; a general having two, one beside the other and a *General-Oberst* having three, one above two others. The rank of *General-Feld-marschall* was denoted by crossed batons within the crescent.

Epaulettes without fringes were worn in the cavalry, *Uhlans* or lancers having the cloth strap and a part within the crescent usually in their facing colour but there were exceptions. For example, the 14th *Uhlans* who had crimson collar cuffs and plastron had yellow cloth on their epaulettes. One year volunteers in the Imperial army had their epaulettes (if they were *Uhlans*) and shoulder straps edged in cord with coloured lines, black for Prussia and a variety or combination of colours for the other states. Where metal shoulder scales were worn (in some Saxon regiments of *Grenadiers*, the 17th and 21st *Uhlans* and 18th *Carabiniers*), the cord binding appeared on the epaulette retaining strap.

The decorative twisted cord shoulder boards worn in *Dienstgrade* or service order were decorated with the same system of ranking for officers as on the full dress epaulettes. The distinctive differences displayed by the lack of, or the abundance of, fringing on the full dress epaulettes was indicated by the way the cording was laid on the board. The lower ranks up to *Hauptmann* had the cord in a series of lines while the middle group had the cord plaited and interwoven. The top ranks, besides the lack of a regimental number also had twisted cord boards but with a coloured edging to the cord. Other ranks' shoulder straps were in a set colour and adorned with the regimental number or approved badge or device; for example, the 3rd Regiment of Guard Grenadiers had red cloth straps embroidered with a crown over 'F.I.' (Franz Imperator) in yellow while the 4th Regiment had light blue with 'A' (Augusta) with the royal crown above, all in red. The 1st Guard Dragoon regiment had Queen Victoria's Imperial crown and cypher, 'V.R.I.' (also used by the British 21st Empress of India's Lancers) to denote that the regiment was '*Konigen Viktoria von Grossbrit. und Irland*'. The 8th *Cuirassiers* had the crown and royal cypher of George V (G.R. V) on their shoulder straps.

In the United States, officers had worn gold lace and fringed epaulettes with metal crescents, shaped and styled after the British fashion. In the regulations issued just prior to the American Civil War enlisted men of the infantry, artillery, engineers and ordnance and hospital stewards were ordered to wear a pair of brass shoulder scales when in full dress. This order also extended to the cavalry and light artillery in the same order or dress; in others the epaulette was not worn. The time-old system of distinguishing rank by means of epaulettes was also used in the American army, the thickness and quality of the fringing aiding identification of various ranks. Major-generals commanding the army had three stars, two large and one small; major-generals had two stars omitting the small one, which brigadier-generals had a single star. For colonels, a silver embroidered spread eagle replaced the star on the strap and within the crescent for the infantry was 'the number of the regiment embroidered in gold, within a circle of embroidered silver' on light- or sky-blue cloth, artillery having scarlet and cavalry yellow. The other corps and departments were distinguished by various badges in place of the Regimental number. The Medical Department had 'M.S.' in Old English within a silver wreath, engineers a turreted castle and ordnance a flaming grenade.

Lieutenant-colonels replaced the eagle on the strap with a silver leaf, while that of major was plain. Captains had less bullion on the fringe and two silver bars while lieutenants had a single bar. Officers below that rank had a plain strap.

When the epaulette was not worn, rank recognition was by means of shoulder straps placed across the shoulder near the top of the arm. These straps had a cloth background depending on the arm of the service, Saxony-blue for infantry, green for rifles, yellow for cavalry and orange for dragoons, etc. These were edged in gold embroidery and bore the same ranking as on the full dress epaulette except that majors had embroidered gold leaves, one at each end. Colonels, captains and lieutenants bore their respective marks of rank, one leaf or bar(s), at each end of the strap.

(f) EQUIPMENT (INFANTRY AND CAVALRY)

The basic equipment of the European foot soldier at the beginning of the eighteenth century was a waistbelt which was fitted with a frog or similar means to suspend a bayonet, usually a plug bayonet or ring bayonet, and a short sword or hanger. Over the left shoulder was worn a cross-belt that fastened on the chest with a brass buckle and from which was suspended a large ammunition box or pouch on the right hip. A knapsack or haversack was also slung across the body by a strap and contained personal belongings, any extra clothing and rations for a march. The combined weight would have been around 50 lb.

The cavalryman's equipment was similar and dictated by the needs of a mounted man; namely, somewhere to carry the sword and a suitable pouch for ammunition for the firelock or pistol. The haversack and other items were, however, carried on the horse.

In the British infantry the practice of wearing the waistbelt over the shoulder for easier access to the sword or bayonet crept in prior to 1750, although this practice was far from general.

By the 1770s white buff cross-belts were being worn by the infantry to carry their weapons and ammunition; and a cow hide knapsack, sometimes made of goat skin, was slung on the back. In addition a grey or buff canvas haversack was slung on the right hip with a tin water-bottle above it. By the time of the Napoleonic wars the knapsack, which had been for the previous few years of canvas, sometimes painted black or other colours and decorated with the regimental badge or number, was replaced by a canvas knapsack with a wood box-like construction on the inside to give it a square appearance. The water-bottle or canteen was now made of wood and was a barrel-like container usually painted blue and bearing the regimental number and that of the man's company. The bayonet cross-belt (swords had been given up in the infantry by 1762) was fastened on the chest by the cross-belt plate, 93 and by cutting one of the ends the belt could be adjusted to fit the soldier. The belt holding the ammunition box fastened to the black leather at each side, with a brass buckle which served as the mode of adjusting the belt.

This basic equipment, with the addition of a 'D'-shaped mess tin in an oilskin cover strapped to the knapsack, continued as the equipment of the foot soldier until the 1850s. Battalions of the Royal Artillery had been ordered to wear a waistbelt with a sword/bayonet frog in 1842 to replace the cross-belt. In 1850 this was gradually introduced for the rest of the infantry with the addition of another black leather ammunition pouch which was worn on the right side of the waistbelt. A small buff leather pouch was fitted to either the cross-belt or the coatee to take the percussion caps for the musket.

In 1871 a new, complete equipment was introduced: the valise equipment, so called because the knapsack with its boxed sides was finally replaced with a valise. The new equipment included a waistbelt with a brass 'D' each side of the locket; to each of these was buckled a strap which passed over the shoulders and crossed in the middle of the back, passing back under the arm and buckling on to the lower part of the opposite strap. To each side of the waistbelt were fitted black leather pouches (except for the Guards and 29th who had white pouches, which the latter adopted in 1877) but these were changed to white buff around 1879–80. The valise was slung on the buttocks attached to the belt and braces with coat, cape and mess tin above. In 1882 an improved valise equipment was introduced which brought back the knapsack, slung slightly higher on the back with the coat and mess tin strapped above. With these last two patterns a black leather 'ball bag' was fitted below the right-hand pouch to contain an extra thirty rounds. When the valise was not worn this could be worn on the belt at the back. In 1875 the wood canteen used since the beginning of the century was replaced by a new pattern. This was like a small upright barrel with a zinc stopper. Holding a quart of water these bottles were mainly manufactured by Guglielminitti Brothers of Turin whose label is often found on the base. The regimental numbers were stamped into the rim at the top.

In 1888 a new pattern of equipment was introduced; designed by Colonel Slade and Lieutenant-Colonel Wallace, it was called the Slade–Wallace equipment. It consisted of a waistbelt which held a bayonet frog on the left and a pouch each side at the front. From behind the pouch, attached to a 'D' on the belt, emerged a shaped shoulder strap which crossed at the back and fastened on to a corresponding 'D' at the back. The mess tin was fastened to the back of the waistbelt over the blanket or greatcoat. The newly designed valise fastened high on the shoulders by straps which passed over the shoulders, through two brass guides sewn to the shoulder staps, and buckled on to the shoulder strap just above the level of the pouch. The old pattern haversack and waterbottle were carried, the latter being replaced prior to 1900 with a round tin one covered in khaki felt.

In 1903, when charger loading was introduced for the army with the new S.M.L.E. rifle, a new equipment was sought. A strong contender had been the Mills equipment which was made of woven webbing; but experiences in the South African War with flimsy emergency bandoliers designed to be thrown away convinced those responsible that leather, and only leather, was the material needed. The new, bandolier equipment consisted of a brown leather waistbelt with two pouches on one side, three the other, and a bandolier containing a further five pouches across the body. The mess tin was carried behind and the waterbottle and haversack, as previously done, on separate cross straps. No pack was carried but the greatcoat was folded and carried high on the shoulders. In 1906 Major Burrows of the 1st Royal Irish Fusiliers put forward the idea of a new pattern of equipment, scientifically distributing the weight carried by the soldier. Through the War Office he collaborated with the Mills Equipment Company which resulted in a completely new web equipment being sanctioned in 1908. The new pattern had a wide web waistbelt and five pouches arranged each side, two over three, and a shoulder brace that fitted behind the pouches, crossed at the back and fastened to the rear of the belt. To the loose ends of the shoulder strap were fastened the waterbottle in a web carrier, and the haversack; the large pack was fastened to brass buckles on the cross braces. An entrenching tool holder was worn beneath the belt at the back. This pattern of equipment was worn throughout the First World War and continued in use until the late 1930s when it was replaced by the 'Pattern 37' equipment.

By the latter years of the eighteenth century the cavalry were wearing a cross-belt similar to that of the infantry, but by the beginning of the nineteenth century these had already started to disappear. In their place a waistbelt was worn to suspend the sword, and a single cross-belt with a black leather pouch was retained and worn over the left shoulder. The white buff leather belt, with brass buckle, slide and tip for adjustment, suspended an iron swivel and hook from the lowest point at the right back, which clipped to the slide on the carbine. Two smaller straps were stitched to the main belt and held a black leather pouch directly above the carbine swivel. This pattern of equipment was retained up until the 1870s when the Martini–Henry carbine without a sling swivel fitted was issued. A leather sheath, which had been provided for some years for the carbine when not slung from the belt, 95 was now the sole means of carrying the weapon. The sling swivel disappeared from the belt which was now a simple affair with a black leather pouch. This belt and pouch were retained until just after the Boer War when it was replaced by a bandolier for service dress in the field and abolished for full dress.

Cavalry officers too had worn a cross-belt and pouch since the early years of the nineteenth century. The belts were in gold or silver lace and adorned with metal ornaments, and the pouches were embroidered with the crown and Royal cypher and ornamentation as on the sabretache. As with the sabretache, battle honours and approved regimental badges started to be included, growing more numerous as the century wore on. By 1846 the Dress Regulations note the following variations for officers' pouches:

Life Guards had a gold lace belt with gilt furniture and a red central line for the 1st and blue for the 2nd with a blue leather covered pouch with velvet flap embroidered in gold. The Royal Horse Guards also had a gold lace belt but with a crimson line and a black leather pouch with gilt regimental badge. In the dragoons and dragoon guard, the cross-belt was in two-inch wide gold lace on leather in the regimental facing colour with a gilt buckle slide and tip. The pouch was covered in leather of the regimental colour, the flat in velvet or cloth of the same colour, edged in gold lace with the edge of the flap showing, and an embroidered 'V.R.' with the crown in silver encircled by oak leaves. The light dragoons' cross-belt was also in gold lace with a central silk stripe, silver buckle slide and tip and silver plates on the front holding two chains and pickers. The pouch was covered in black leather with gold embroidered on the top edge and with a solid silver flap engraved around the edge and bearing a mounted, crowned 'V.R.' in gilt brass. The lancers wore a similar cross-belt with silver furniture and a silver-fronted pouch covered in scarlet leather (the 9th and 17th had blue leather covering) with the raised gilt brass crowned Royal cypher. The 8th displayed the double 'A.R.' cypher as on their lance cap plates.

Hussars, except for the 10th, had gold lace cross-belts with gilt buckle slide and tip showing a scarlet edge each side, and a scarlet cloth pouch edged in gold lace and decorated with embroidery. In the 11th, the edging of the belt and covering of a special pattern pouch with gilt flap and silver ornaments were in crimson. In the 10th Hussars, the belt and pouch were in black leather and decorated with gilt criss-cross ornaments and the regimental badge.

By the time of the Crimean War, the 9th Lancers had gilt fittings to their cross-belts and had adopted a crimson-covered pouch with gilt

Verlag u. Druck v. L. Sachse & C?. Berlin.

46.

2⁺ Dragoner Rgt. – 3⁺ Ulanen Rgt. – 3⁺ Artillerie Br. – 6⁺ Cuir. Rgt. – 3⁺ Husaren Rgt.

19. Print of the Prussian Cavalry circa *1843 showing the various uniforms of each arm*

20. Private of the British 13th Hussars in service dress as worn throughout the First World War

21. Private of the German 113th Infantry Regiment in waffenrock *1914*

flap of a distinctive shape with raised border and crowned double 'A.R.' cypher in the centre.

When the Household Cavalry and heavy cavalry gave up the embroidered sabretaches in 1854 the former adopted one in black patent leather with regimental device on the flap while the heavy cavalry adopted a silver flap pouch ornamented with the royal cypher in gilt with crown above.

In other European countries the cross-belt arrangement for the infantryman was also widely adopted but usually without a cross-belt plate, a simple brass buckle sufficing. In France, the cross-belt pattern of equipment was discontinued by troops during the war in Algeria and the colonisation of parts of North Africa; but the troops at home continued to wear the cross-belts until 1845 when Regulations introduced a completely new uniform and equipment. Trials had been made in various regiments prior to 1845 as a result of which the cartouche box was reduced in size and fitted to either the back or front of a waist-belt which also supported a bayonet and hanger on the left side. The cow-hide or calf skin *havre-sac* was worn on the back with straps passing over the shoulder and under the arms, and with the greatcoat in a ticking bag fitted to the top. The tunic could be packed into this bag when only the greatcoat was worn, a practice which originated in the Algerian campaign and became increasingly popular. The various supporting straps can be clearly seen in Plate 53. While the French paid close attention to the fashion aspect of their uniforms and shakos little was done with regard to the equipment. The basic 1845 pattern survived until after the Franco–Prussian War. Presumably no change was required as the equipment seemed to be properly designed; the pack being supported on the back and held in place by supporting straps which fastened to the front of the waistbelt, and the single ammunition pouch worn either at the back or front.

About 1886, when the Lebel rifle was introduced, the large single ammunition box was found to be inconvenient and unsuitable. In its place two pouches were issued, worn one each side of the waistbelt at the front. This remained the basic French equipment up to and including the First World War. Even after the 1920s there was no apparent need to change it and it was still being worn by the *Poilus* in 1940.

The cavalry wore a similar arrangement to that used in Britain; those troops armed with carbines had the sling swivel to the belt while those with pistols wore a belt with pouch only.

In Prussia the cross-belt equipment lasted until 1847 when a waistbelt with supporting braces for the knapsack was introduced. As in the French army, the ammunition pouch could be worn at either the back or the front. Until 1850 the equipment was in white leather but after that date black was almost universally adopted. In the 1860s, the single ammunition pouch was replaced by two pouches worn either side at the front. They were attached to the belt by loops and hung down below the level of the belt. In 1911 these pouches were abolished and in their place were issued six smaller pouches which fitted three on either side of the waistbelt. The cavalry, who up until 1911 had worn the almost universal cross-belt and pouch, adopted an equipment with waistbelt and braces together with ammunition pouches similar to that worn by the infantry.

In Prussia, as in other countries, cavalry officers wore an ornate cross-belt and pouch. In the Imperial German army the cross-belts were in lace, usually decorated with two plates on the front holding chain and pickers or with a shield bearing a State or particular regimental badge. The *Jäger zu Pferde* for example had two plates, the upper bearing the Prussian eagle with 'F.R.' on its breast and the lower one a crowned 'W'. There was a single picker fitted to the left side of the lower plate.

The pouches were either in black patent leather or with metal flaps. The *Garde du Corps* had a black pouch with the Guard star on the flap while line regiments of Prussia, Oldenburg and Baden had the crowned cypher of Frederick the Great on the flap. There were, of course, exceptions. The 1st *Cuirassiers* had the so-called eagle of Frederick the Great within a crowned wreath while the 2nd had the Prussian eagle surmounted on a trophy of flags and cannon with a grenade in each lower corner of the flap. The King's *Jäger zu Pferde* officers had a metal flap to the pouch with a crowned bugle horn motif with the cypher of Frederick the Great in the centre. Saxon and Bavarian officers bore the State arms on the metal flaps of the pouch.

Other ranks had larger and squarer black ammunition pouches. Those of the Prussian line had a plain flap; the 1st *Cuirassiers* had the eagle of Frederick the Great in a plain circle, and the 2nd *Cuirassiers* had the line eagle over the trophy similar to that of the officers but again in a plain circle with two grenades in the lower corners of the flap. The N.C.O.s of the 23rd and 24th Dragoons had the crowned letter 'L' on the flap, the other ranks having a plain flap without badge.

The method of carrying the knapsack varied from country to country. Most, in the early part of the nineteenth century, were slung on the back by straps over the shoulder and under the arm; but even in this position, unless the straps were very tight, the pack would be liable to move when the men were marching or on campaign. In Britain, as in Prussia and Austria, this movement was stopped or lessened by the chest connecting strap which fastened to each shoulder brace just by the armpit and buckled across the chest. In Prussia the strap was fairly low down but in Britain and other countries it was high up. It had to be buckled so tight to stop any movement, that it constricted the chest and made movement after a time painful. This resulted in it often being left undone on marches. An eminent general, Sir William Butler, wrote in his memoirs published in 1911 that the wearing of the pack with the tight connecting strap broke the health of many men before they were forty. The French did not use a connecting strap to their shoulder braces.

In Prussia, France and other countries, this mode of carrying the pack disappeared in the 1840s and '50s as the new equipments mentioned above were introduced. In Britain, the connecting strap survived until the valise equipment of 1871. In Russia, the knapsack straps were supported on the waistbelt from an early date. This can be seen in Plate 94.

In the United States, by the time of the Civil War, the cross-belt with ammunition box was used in conjunction with a waistbelt which held the bayonet, and a small pouch for the percussion caps. The pack was held by shoulder straps and the infamous connecting chest strap. In the cavalry a black leather cross-belt was worn to hold the carbine swivel, a waistbelt to hold the sword, a holster for a revolver and a pouch for ammunition.

In 1880 the United States army adopted the canvas web equipment patented in 1899 by Captain Anson Mills. This at first consisted of a waistbelt and shoulder belt with loops to hold the ammunition, together with a wrist belt holding a few rounds for immediate use. By the time the Americans had adopted a smaller calibre rifle belts with a double layer of loops were in use. By the first decade of the twentieth century, the Americans had adopted a complete web equipment for the army. Revolver and sword belts were designed in the same material for cavalry (it was still the time of the mounted cavalryman), packs and a host of other items. This 1910 equipment is still basically that worn today by the American army although progress in weapons and experience in war has made many modifications in its design.

(g) CUIRASSES

Besides the gorget, the cuirass was another piece of armour to survive the radical change in warfare and uniforms brought about by the general introduction of firearms. At first, this added protection for the heavy cavalryman was adequate proof against the musket balls; but as the muskets became more streamlined and their design more advanced the cuirass was only useful as protection at a distance. As the cavalry role was to get to grips with the opposing infantry and 'bulldoze' them off the field by sheer weight and force, the cuirass was considered by some countries to be superfluous, only adding to the weight and, therefore, slowing the speed of the heavy cavalryman.

Britain was one of the first to discard the cuirass. By 1707 cuirasses were being worn only by regiments of horse and then, it seems, only the breastplate in an effort to increase mobility and reduce weight. By 1714 the regiments of horse were already handing in the breastplates to the Tower and in 1717 the Board of Ordnance ordered that:

> April 8. Delivered to be sold by auction . . . Helmets 136, Backs with culettes 602, Backs without culettes 529, Backs unserviceable 236, Brests repaired 371, Potts repaired 1084 . . .

Towards the end of the century most, if not all, of the breastplates and other items mentioned above had been disposed of or were utilised in the making of large decorations. These hung on the walls of Hampton Court and brightened the otherwise dismal appearance of the inside of the Grand Storehouse in the Tower, the main depot for military arms and equipment.

In 1820, on the occasion of the coronation of George IV who had for some years held the position of Regent and who had introduced into the army the 'fashion race' that prevailed amongst civilians during his era, the Household Cavalry consisting of the two regiments of Life Guards and the Royal Horse Guards were issued with cuirasses. None of these were of the old style that might have been still in store, but were an entirely new manufacture. The obvious influence of the Royal Guard of the French monarch can be clearly seen in the new plates. These were in silvered metal, edged in gilt beading and studs and edged for the two Life Guards in blue and for the Royal Horse Guards in red. On the front of the breast was fitted a large, gilt, oval, engraved plate on a star of rays. This decorative badge lasted until 1825 when it disappeared leaving the breastplate as plain as it is today. Except for minor variations in size and shape, the cuirass is still part of the full dress of officers and other ranks of the Household Cavalry.

In Europe other countries, notably France and Prussia, persisted in having their heavy cavalry or *Cuirassiers* wear the heavy steel cuirass. France retained this item as part of fighting dress up until the first years of the First World War, and Prussian *Cuirassiers* after 1880 preserved the breastplate and back-plate for parade wear only. The French pattern made of steel had brass shoulder scales and a belt attached to the back-plate which fastened over the bottom of the breastplate. The lining extended beyond the edge of the metal and was gathered around the armholes, down the sides and along the bottom. The *Carabiniers* were equipped with brassed cuirasses in 1809 to match their helmets while the *Cent Garde* formed by Napoleon III followed the example of previous Royal Guards in having a brass or gilt brass badge and star on the front of the breastplate.

In 1814 Prussian *Cuirassiers* were wearing the captured brassed cuirasses of the *Carabiners* which they exchanged for steel in 1821. On special and important occasions the *Garde du Corps* wore blackened cuirasses that had been presented to them by the Russian Emperor Alexander I and which were exactly the same as those worn by the guard and line *Cuirassiers* in Russia up until 1846.

In Russia and Prussia the Royal Guard, or *Garde du Corps*, were provided with 'supervestes' which in shape resembled the cuirass and usually bore a metal or embroidered badge on the chest. That of the Prussian *Garde du Corps* can be seen in Plate 65.

4: Colours and drums

(a) COLOURS

Even before the use of uniform clothing which distinguished individual regiments and opposing armies, regimental colours, flags, etc, were in widespread use in the fighting forces of Europe. From Roman times standards had been used as a rallying point for troops and were respected and venerated by the soldiers, a feeling which is still alive today concerning a regiment's colour.

In Britain, as in most countries, the proprietary system whereby the regiment was very much the personal property of the colonel was in vogue. Naturally the device borne on the regiment's colours would be his and those of his officers who commanded the various companies. For example The Queen's Majesty's Regiment of Foot (later 4th Foot, the King's Own Royal Regiment) whose colonel during the time of James II was Colonel Charles Trelawny, bore on the lieutenant-colonel's colour the crest of the D.Este family. Sir William Clifton's regiment bore on the colonel's colour the Clifton crest, a demi-peacock issuing from a ducal coronet, while the colours of the lieutenant-colonel, major and senior captain bore another Clifton crest, i.e. cinque-foils.

As the colonels changed, either through death or because the regiment was 'sold' to another, the crests on the colours altered. Royal regiments bore on their colours the royal badges of members of the Royal Family, a practice widely adopted for royal troops in other European countries.

In Britain the first Royal Warrant to lay down details of the colours to be supplied to the bodyguard regiments of Charles II after his restoration was the warrant issued at 'our Court in Whitehall this 13th day of February, 1661', which stated that:

> . . . we do hereby require you forthwith to cause to be made and provided, twelve colours or ensigns for Our Regiment of Foot Guards, of white and red taffeta, of the usual largeness, with stands, heads and tassels, each of which to have such distinctions of some of our Royal Badges, painted in oil, as our trusty and well-beloved servant Sir Edward Walker, Knight Garter Principal King-at-Arms, shall direct . . .

Personal colours continued in use during the early part of the eighteenth century but the number per regiment was reduced to three in about

1707; one for the centre division of pikes and one each for flank divisions, musketeers and grenadiers. When pikes were abolished soon after, the colours of a regiment numbered only two. This is how it is to this day, except with regiments who have an 'honoury' colour.

The first set of regulations that detailed exactly what should be borne on a regiment's colours, and abolished the long tradition of personal crests and devices were 'Regulations for the colours of the marching regiments, 1747, as delivered to the Clothing Board, November 11th 1749; Robert Napier, Adjutant-General.' These were supplemented with a coloured drawing of each colour showing the size, shape and position of the devices borne on them.

The regulations stated that:

> No Colonel to put his Arms, Crest, Device or Livery on any part of the Appointments of the Regiment under his command.
>
> No part of the Cloathing or Ornaments of the Regiments to be altered, after the following Regulations are put into execution but by His Majesty's permission.

It is well worth quoting the description of the colours which forms the basis of the design till the present day.

> The KING'S or FIRST COLOUR of every Regiment or Battalion is to be the GREAT UNION. The SECOND COLOUR to be the colour of the Faceing of the Regiment with the Union in the Upper canton, except those Regiments which are faced White or Red, whose Second Colour is to be the Red-Cross of St. George on a White ground and the Union in the upper canton. In the center of each Colour is to be painted or embroidered in gold Roman characters the number of the Rank of the Regiment within a Wreath of Roses and Thistles on the same stalk; except the Regiments which have Royal Badges or particular ancient Badges allowed them; in these the number of the Rank of the Regiment is to be towards the upper corner . . . The Cords and Tassels of all Colours to be Crimson the Gold.

A Royal Warrant was issued in 1751 based on that of 1747 and except for minor unimportant changes in the wording describes the colours in the same way. For the first time, standards and guidons are mentioned for dragoon guards and Standards for Regiments of horse. Dragoons' guidons were also described.

Whereas the infantry colours were allowed to be painted or embroidered, standards and guidons were to be:

> . . . of Damask embroidered and fringed with Gold or Silver. The Guidons of the Regts of Dragoons to be of silk, the tassels and cords of the whole to be of crimson silk and gold mixed . . .

The King's or First Standard, or Guidon of each Regiment to be crimson with the Rose and Thistle conjoined, and Crown over them, in the centre His Majesty's Motto, Dieu et mon Droit, underneath, the White Horse in a Compartment, in the first and fourth corners, and the rank of the Regiment, in gold or silver characters, on a ground of the same colour as the faceing of the Regiment in a compartment in the second and third corners.

The second colour was in the facing colour of the regiment with the badge of the regiment in the centre, or its rank in roman characters on a crimson ground within a rose and thistle wreath. Beneath was the regimental motto with the white horse in the first and fourth compartment, and rose and thistle in the second and third. The third standard or guidon was similar to that described above but the warrant stated that:

The Distinction of the Third Standard or Guidon to be a Figure on a circular ground of red underneath the Motto.

The first mention of any battle honours being borne on standards or colours occurs in the 1768 Warrant. In the 'general view' four new light dragoon regiments are mentioned, amongst them the 15th who were granted the motto *Emsdorff* for their conduct at the battle (16th July 1760).

In 1801 the political union of Great Britain and Ireland was effected by an Order in Council which made a change in the 'Great Union' with the introduction of the red cross of St. Patrick and the inclusion of the shamrock with the rose and thistle in the union wreath. Some colours, we are told, were converted if they were in good condition while others were withdrawn and new ones issued.

After 1830, when silver lace was abolished for the regular army, standards were fringed in crimson and gold, and the embroidery was in gold wire only. Light dragoons had ceased to carry standards by Horse Guard letter of May 1834.

In 1844 infantry regiments were ordered by the Regulation of that year to place their title, either royal or county, on the colours and at the same time it was stipulated that battle honours, badges, etc, were to be placed on the regimental third and fourth standards and regimental colours only.

In 1857 the size of regimental colours was reduced from 6 ft. 6 in. flying and 6 ft. deep on the pike to 6 ft. flying and 5 ft. 6 in. deep. Two years later dragoon guards and dragoons were ordered to carry one standard or guidon per regiment. In the same 'Queen's Regulation and Orders for the Army', second battalions were to be distinguished by 'II BATT' beneath the union wreath and colours were again reduced in size; this time to 4 ft. flying and 3 ft. 6 in. deep. They were also to be fringed with crimson and gold. In 1868 colours were again reduced; this time to the size they are today, 3 ft. 9 in. flying and 3 ft. deep. The pike now bore on the top in place of a spear head a gilt royal crest, and in 1873 was reduced from 9 ft. 10 in. to 8 ft. 7½ in.

In 1881 the Cardwell reform system took effect and linked regiments into two battalion regiments with county or royal titles, sweeping away the 'number' system. All English regiments were to be faced white, Scottish yellow and Irish green, except royal regiments which retained blue. This made a radical change in the regimental colour which now appeared without the union in the upper canton. The new regimental and Queen's colours were to have 'the territorial designation *if practicable* to be inscribed on a circle . . .'

After the First World War clothing regulations Part 1 authorised battle honours to be placed on the King's colour, a practice that had ceased in 1844.

In other countries, colours or standards had the same importance and significance as in Britain. In France the Royalist army prior to the French Revolution had two types of colours authorised by Louis XIV in 1671: a white one reserved for the colonel's troops and another with a white cross for battalions and companies. The cavalry, however, did not have a uniform standard, preferring instead to display the arms of the town or province in which they were raised. The fleur de lis, an emblem adopted in the Middle Ages, was always much in evidence on French colours and standards up until the Revolution.

In Russia the double-headed eagle adopted after the marriage of Ivan III to Sophia, heiress of the last Byzantine emperor, was a widely featured symbol on colours and flags. During the eighteenth century a similar emblem of a double-headed eagle was adopted by both Austria and Hungary, this being the ancient symbol of the Hapsburgs. Prussia often used the black eagle and monogram of Frederick the Great on the various colours and standards of the Prussian army and featured it widely on the flags of the unified German Empire, on which it appeared in the centre against a background of white and encircled with a crowned laurel wreath. A large number of Prussian colours were distinguished by an 'X' superimposed on the basic colour but with each arm of the cross tapering towards the central symbol. Holland employed the lion of Nassau, while Poland utilised the outspread eagle. In Denmark at the beginning of the eighteenth century a large coat of arms was borne on the colours with a white cross on a red ground in the upper canton while in Sweden at the same period the crowned monogram and cypher of the king with supporters was much in evidence.

After the French Revolution the royalist colours were dispensed with and the national flag adopted. In 1804 with the creation of the *Grande Armée* and the proclamation of an Empire by Napoleon the Emperor ordered new colours for the entire army. These took the form of the national flag, fringed in gold and embroidered with the name of the regiment, and any battle honours or designation conferred by the Emperor. The most striking part of the new colours or standards was the gilt eagle with outstretched wings that surmounted the pole giving the name of 'the eagles' by which the colours were referred to. French army colours are today still the tricolour with the name of the regiment embroidered on it. Besides distinctions of battle honours, ribbons tied to the top testify to a regiment's gallantry in a certain action or war.

In America, during the revolutionary war, the continental army used firstly the grand union but this was quickly changed for the Stars and Stripes which was a national flag supplemented by regimental and divisional colours. The American grand union had thirteen alternate red and white stripes with the union flag in the upper canton. On 14th June 1777 Congress resolved 'that the flag of the United States be made of thirteen stripes, alternate red and white; that the union be thirteen stars, white in a blue field . . .' In May 1775 standards were ordered for the army of Connecticut which were to be:

. . . for the First yellow, the Second blue, the Third scarlet, Fourth crimson, the Fifth white, and the Sixth azure.

However, because of the unavailability of blue cloth the colour and facings of the Second regiment were changed to green. Blue was given to the Seventh regiment when it was raised and orange to the Eighth. These regimental colours usually bore various designs upon them, plus mottoes. The divisional colours also bore some distinction of the regiment either in motto, motif or colour but their exact design is unknown.

In 1779 it was decided that each regiment should have two colours to bear the regimental number in gold on a blue garter: the first to be the flag of the United States and the second to be a regimental colour in the facing of the regiment.

Just prior to the American Civil War colours were described in the 1864 regulations. Garrison flags were to be the National flag while camp colours were described as being eighteen inches square, white for the infantry, red for the artillery, each bearing the number of the regiment. Unlike the British artillery who did not carry colours, their guns being their colours, the American artillery had two colours per regiment. The first was the national 'Stars and Stripes' embroidered on the central stripe with the regiment's name, while the second was ordered to be:

. . . yellow, of the same dimensions as the first, bearing in the centre two cannons crossing, with the letters U.S. above, and the number of the regiment below. Each colour to be six feet six inches fly, and six feet deep on the pike.

The cords and tassels that adorned the top of the 9 ft. 10 in. pike were red and yellow silk mixed.

The infantry had a national colour and a regimental one, the latter in blue with the arms of the United States embroidered on it. The name of the regiment was placed on a scroll beneath the eagle. The size was the same as for the artillery colour.

In the cavalry each regiment was ordered a standard and each company a guidon. The standard was blue embroidered with the arms of the United States and the regimental number and name in a scroll beneath the eagle. The dimensions were 2 ft. 5 in. wide and 2 ft. 3 in. deep. The guidon was swallowtailed, as it was in other armies, and was half red and half white. On the upper red portion were the letters U.S. in white, and on the white the letter of the company in red.

(b) DRUMS

In the 1751 Regulations 'for the uniform CLOATHING of the MARCHING REGIMENTS . . .' the drums were ordered to be emblazoned in like manner to the Bell of Arms which itself was directed to have '. . . THE KING'S CYPHER AND CROWN and the number of the Regiment under it painted on a ground of the same colour as the facings of the Regiment'. Those regiments entitled, i.e. the Royal regiments and the 'six Old Corps' were allowed to emblazon their approved badges.

The cavalry had kettle drums which were draped with banners and these were to be in the facing colour of the regiment with either its badge or number in the centre. During the nineteenth century as various battle honours were awarded these drum banners became very crowded.

In the infantry the drums were also emblazoned with battle honours and approved badges (see Plate 126) in profusion; some regiments even going to the expense, which was borne by the officers, of having silver drums with raised coat of arms, title and battle honours.

Most of the larger drums, such as bass and tenor drums, were made of wood while the majority of the side drums were made either in brass or white metal. During the latter years of the ninteenth century these were emblazoned, if desired, at the regiment's expense. 'Ordnance issue' drums as they were known were usually in plain brass with red, white and blue hoops, white ropes and tensioners, except for rifle regiments who had green and black hoops, black cords and tensioners. However, not all regiments had the plain red, white and blue hoops, others preferring a design particular to them or commemorating a   107 certain battle or action. The 5th Northumberland Fusiliers had white and green vandyked hoops to commemorate drums captured from the Russians in the Crimea (that design of hoop being popular on brass Russian military side drums). The South Wales Borderers who also adopted green and white vandyked hoops at the beginning of this century did it, it seems, from purely personal choice, having no connection with the Crimean campaign.

In America, drums for the infantry tended to follow the same design as laid down for colours, namely a blue background with the arms of the United States emblazoned in the middle with a scroll bearing the regimental name. The hoops on side drums at this period for infantry were red.

In Russia, side drums at the time of the Crimean War were in brass and impressed from the back with the double eagle emblem. This badge was also impressed on military bugles. In Denmark brass drums with either badge or national crest impressed from the back were in use in the early 1700s, while in Sweden drums of this period were invariably emblazoned with the royal cypher of the reigning monarch. By the 1820s the side drum became shallower and somewhat similar to that in vogue in Prussia, although deeper brass drums with the crowned cypher of the reigning monarch displayed in a circle on a trophy of arms and flags were still much in evidence.

In Prussia the shallow side drum was most popular and was distinctive in that it had a vandyked hoop and little or no decoration on the brass shell itself. Even before 1871 and the creation of the Imperial German Empire this style of drum seems to have spread amongst the various armies of the German states, the colours of the hoops in their distinctive vandyked pattern showing either a regimental or state distinction. In France side drums tended to be plain and even those of the infantry were draped with regimental banners, a practice still continued to this day.

Drum majors in most countries not only carried a decorative mace that was adorned with national or regimental symbols and battle honours but also wore a cross-belt which was ornamented with the national or regimental badge and garnished with two silver or gilt-tipped drum sticks in a plate holder.

In Britain during the latter part of the nineteenth century the ordance issue sash bore the regiment's number and any distinctive badge on a cloth of the regimental facing colour, and was trimmed in gold lace. Many regiments preferred to have, at their own expense, a more lavish version which bore the regiment's battle honours, its number and badge, etc. By the time of the institution of the territorial title system in 1881 ordnance issue sashes bore the crowned royal cypher, the regiment's name in a scroll and a pair of drum sticks. In most regiments these sashes were used for less important occasions and when rehearsing, the more elaborate and ornate version being retained for ceremonials. A sash of the Northumberland Fusiliers is shown in Plate 124.

5: Curios

This chapter embraces all those items with military connotations connected with the armies of Europe and America. Some of these items were 'official' such as commissions, pay books and regimental returns, while others were made commercially to sell to a popular market. In Germany beer *steins* painted with military scenes were highly popular, as were the china pipe bowls bearing military scenes or patriotic portraits of the Kaiser. In Britain the Boer War brought forth a mass of items such as medallions, metal or china statues of 'The Gentleman in Khaki', ink stands in the form of military figures or helmets, which all helped to swell the militarism that swept Europe in the late nineteenth and early twentieth centuries. Recruiting posters, discharge papers and even song sheets are all collected for their military association. The items are extremely varied and the scope almost limitless. One of the most popular hobbies is the collecting of military post cards, a great profusion of which were published at the turn of the century by Gale & Polden and Messrs. Raphael Tuck, to name but two. Military cigarette cards also enjoy a large following.

In Britain officers' commissions were always signed by the reigning monarch except in the case of artillery and engineer officers who, prior to 1855 and the dissolution of the Board of Ordnance, had their commissions signed by the Master General of the Ordnance. Although interesting documents, commissions are of little practical value to the historian or researcher as an officer's career can usually be found in potted form in regimental histories, various editions of the Army List and, for East India Company Officers, in Dodwell, and Miles Army List. Soldiers' discharge papers have, however, a practical value for the historian as they recount the entire service of the soldier including whether he gained any medals, good conduct pay, etc. It also serves as an indication of where he did his service and the reason for his discharge. Soldiers' pay books are also of value as they not only give the years of service and date of joining but are usually combined with the pay account to give a useful insight into life in the army, cost of clothing, messing, etc, plus any gratuities awarded for a brave deed or in connection with a medal, such as the Distinguished Conduct Medal.

Other items of interest are identification tags which were worn around the neck and bore the name, rank, number and regiment of the wearer.

The personal identification of the soldier is a fairly recent innovation. During the Boer War a glazed calico card, 'Army Form B 2067, Description Card for Active Service', bore the name, rank and regiment, and name and address of next of kin. It was sewn inside the tunic on the bottom front, right-hand side. During the early nineteenth century recognition was purely visual and losses of men calculated purely by verifying the muster rolls. Individual graves were also unheard of and after Waterloo, for example, mass graves were dug and bodies of men and horses interred together—still in their uniforms, if the looters who scoured the field during the night after the battle had left any. Incidentally, survivors of Waterloo were ordered to be 'enrolled on the muster rolls and pay-lists of their respective corps as *Waterloo-men*', a distinction that was reckoned as two years service towards increase in pay or pension. On discharge papers as late as the Crimea and after the printed form contained a line especially for recording presence at the battle.

Besides the vast amount of official forms, papers and printed drill and regulation books there was the mass of unofficial paraphernalia put out commercially. Cigarette cards and post cards were a popular form of collecting and are eagerly sought after. Gale & Polden, who also produced numerous wall charts of military badges, etc, produced a vast quantity of post cards; their most famous series being 'History and Tradition' which bear in colour a picture of either officer and soldier or soldiers of the regiment, a brief potted history, battle honours and badge. Even with this set it is often possible to find two or even three variations of a particular regiment. The card featuring the Welsh Guards is extremely rare and those of the Yeomanry are particularly hard to find. The illustrations on the cards are by well-known military artists such as Ibbotson and Harry Payne. Another series, not dissimilar, was put out by the same firm entitled 'Soldiers Pay' which gave the brief details of service pay, conditions of enlistment, etc. These too are accompanied by fine colour reproductions of Ibbotson or Payne pictures.

Cigarette cards are another popular area, one which John Player, Gallagher, Carreras and Ogden were only too eager to fill. Those by Player are probably the finest, their 'Head-dress' series being particularly attractive while other series, although well executed, are full of errors. Cigarette cards were not an exclusively British hobby and a particularly fine large set of cards of the army, navy, foreign service and colonial troops of Imperial Germany was put out by Waldorf cigarettes together with a well laid out album which gave additional information on army corps details as well as where each regiment was stationed.

Although virtually unknown in Britain until 1885, cigarette cards soon gathered momentum with the various small rival firms that then existed, each trying to outdo the other with splendid colour series of flowers, actresses and, of course, military uniforms and heroes. The Boer War gave the cigarette manufacturers just what they needed and soon such sets as 'Heroes of the Transvaal War' put out by Salmon and Gluckstein Ltd., the 'South African' series by Gallagher, and Ogden's series of pictures from the war were available. Victoria Cross deeds were also popular and Player put out a series, as did Gallagher, while Wills had their 'Heroic Deeds' series. After the First World War, 'War Decorations and Medals' by Player was extremely popular, as was their mammoth set of Divisional signs. Probably the last military sets produced were two well-executed sets put out by Player in 1938 and 1939: 'Military Uniforms of the British Empire' and 'Uniforms of the Territorial Army'. Cigarette cards disappeared during the Second World War and never re-appeared.

Recruiting posters are another source of information and insight into army life and conditions. An early poster of the Seaforth Highlanders (1784) calls on 'ALL LADS of *True Highland Blood* willing to shew their Loyalty and Spirit' to present themselves at Head Quarters where, the poster states, 'they will receive HIGH BOUNTIES and SOLDIER-LIKE ENTERTAINMENT'. The poster ends with the phrase 'Now for a stroke at the *Monsieurs* my Boys! King George for ever! HUZZA!'

Contemporary French recruiting posters were usually of finer quality, with printed pictures of the uniform in colour. But, as with the British poster, it is only the so-called advantages such as high pay, agreeable surroundings and light service, etc, that are emphasised. After the Waterloo campaign and the peace recruiting posters fell into disuse. During the American Civil War some rather uninspired examples were produced calling on volunteers to enlist. The only incentive offered seems to have been 'Clothes and Rations furnished immediately on being Mustered in'.

Recruiting posters in Britain during the latter years of the nineteenth century usually had a coloured picture showing the uniforms of the regiment, its honours and achievements plus details of service and advantages such as a reading-room, free education and games. Usually 'good prospects of promotion for intelligent and well-conducted men' was offered as the incentive.

The First World War really gave the recruiting poster a front place in importance, all countries eagerly pouring out hundreds of variations. At first they appealed to patriotic feelings but, when that was exhausted, turned to sentiment and, perhaps more dangerous and sinister, near-accusations of cowardice if you didn't join. The famous British poster which came out after an initial, rather staid Press campaign was 'Your Country Needs You' by Alfred Leete, depicting Lord Kitchener pointing

22. Private of the French 60th
Infantry Regiment in horizon-blue
uniform and steel helmet 1916

23. Private of the French 27th
Infantry Regiment in service dress
1914

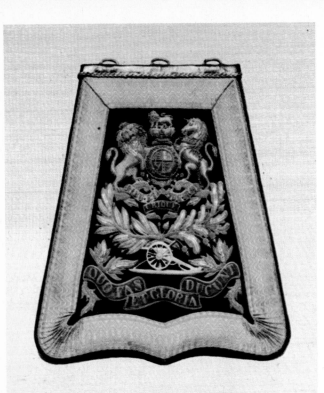

24. *Officer's sabretache of the Royal Artillery* circa *1850*

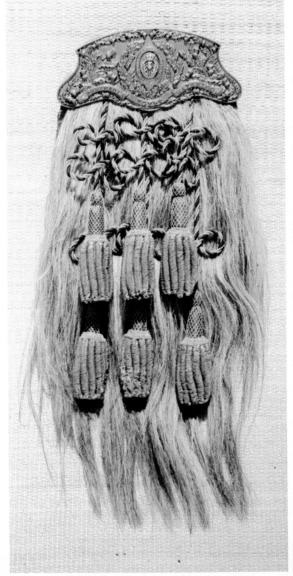

25. *Full dress sporran of the Cameron Highlanders* circa *1905*

directly at you. America followed with their portrait of 'Uncle Sam' in almost the same pose stating 'I want you for the U.S. Army'. Posters were not only aimed at recruiting but, probably of equal importance, they tried to persuade the population to invest their money in war loan or similar bonds.

With conscription becoming general in all armies, recruiting posters, which had now got to the level of 'It is far better to face the bullets than to be killed at home by a bomb—Join the army at once and help to stop an air raid', gave way to war loan posters which in turn were supplemented by the Red Cross and the Salvation Army. Then, when submarine warfare threatened Britain and the Royal Navy blockaded Germany, there were posters about not wasting food or materials.

In Germany one of the most popular forms of military souvenir or curio was the beer *stein*. These coloured drinking mugs were painted with some military scene, usually depicting troops in action, while smaller vignettes showed pictures of enjoyable camp life and usually contained at least one showing the soldier in walking-out dress with his sweetheart. The name of the regiment is painted across the top together with the names of the various men in the owner's company, his own name and dates of serving being added either at the top or base of the mug. Depending on which arm of the service, the pewter top is usually decorated with a soldier on foot for infantry, a mounted man for cavalry, a field gun for artillery and so on. China pipe bowls were decorated in a similar fashion. Collectors should beware of modern reproductions which circulate today. These can usually be recognised as the entire design is transferred on, whereas on genuine pieces only part of the design was so fixed, the owner and his regiment usually being painted on by hand and the various scenes hand coloured.

Drinking vessels and jugs were also popular in Britain but these were usually the 'Toby jug' style in the form of a famous person, such as Kitchener or Lord Roberts, or ordinary jugs depicting a battle scene. While on the subject of painted china, British officers' mess plates can usually be found. They are normally of good quality china and bear the badge of the regiment in the centre. Silver salt cellars and mustard pots can be found, also engraved with regimental badges.

Items made by prisoners of war are also popular, the most sought after being those made by French prisoners during the Napoleonic wars. Usually in the form of sailing ships or cradles, they are made from bone, wood and straw. The authorities allowed the prisoners to sell these to earn money to augment their diet or to buy tobacco. During the First World War German prisoners in Britain also engaged in this sort of work. An example of a medallion in an inlaid box made on the Isle of Man is illustrated in Plate 122.

Shell cases were another material for making souvenirs and items for sale during the First World War. Many shell cases were turned into coffee pots, sugar bowls and ashtrays by troops at the front or, more usually, by the wounded and disabled in hospital. Some are very crudely made while others show fine craftsmanship. In Germany similar items were made, the most prolific being picture frames made from bullets, decorated with small crude enamel copies of medals and pictures of the Kaiser and his generals. An example of this type of work, an ashtray in the form of a cap made from an 18-pounder shell, is illustrated in Plate 122.

Two curios or souvenirs often encountered by collectors are Queen Victoria's chocolate box, presented to troops during the Boer War in 1900 and Princess Mary's Gift, distributed to troops for Christmas 1914. Queen Victoria had ordered a quantity of knitting to be sent to the troops but it appears that only the officers benefited from this gesture. Accordingly, 100,000 tins of chocolate were ordered from Fry's, Rowntree's and Cadbury's, packed in specially designed tins. The bottom of the tin was gold in colour and the lid had a red background with a gilt medallion in the centre bearing the Queen's head. On the left was the crowned Imperial cypher 'V.R.I.' and on the right 'South Africa 1900'. Along the base in facsimile of the Queen's handwriting ran the message 'I wish you a happy New Year. Victoria R.I.' The box is more often than not found empty but can still be found with the bars of chocolate and shredded paper packing. The boxes with the Cadbury's and Rowntree's chocolate were the same size, and the Fry's box slightly larger.

For Christmas 1914 a fund was launched to provide gifts for every man wearing the King's uniform on Christmas day, nurses at the front, widows or parents of men killed, prisoners and interned men. The gift took the form of a brass box with embossed lid bearing the head of the Princess Mary in relief, with the words 'Imperium Britannicum' above and 'Christmas 1914' below. At the sides and corners were the names of the Allies: France, Russia, Belgium, Japan, Serbia and Montenegro. The recipients were divided into classes and the gifts varied accordingly. Group A consisting of the Navy and troops in France received the box, a pipe, an ounce of tobacco, a packet of cigarettes, a pencil made from a bullet, a Christmas card and a picture of Princess Mary. Boys received the box and a Christmas card while non-smokers received a packet of acid drops in lieu of the tobacco and cigarettes. Indian troops received the gift too; Sikhs having the box filled with sugar candy and in addition a tin box of spices while other troops received the tobacco and cigarettes. The tobacco and 20 cigarettes were packed in a special yellow wrapper bearing the monogram of H.R.H. Princess Mary with the date and name of the fund. It is often possible to find the box complete with cigarettes, tobacco, portrait and Christmas card, but far rarer are those which contain the packet of acid drops or the chocolate which was supplied to nurses at the front. The same colour and design of wrapper was used on both the latter mentioned gifts.

The items that come under the heading of curios are so numerous that not every facet can be discussed. The more usual have been mentioned above but items such as military orders, military mail and siege or occupation money can be considered by the general collector as coming under the heading of curios. Military mail and siege money are only a small facet of other hobbies and they are of passing interest only to the collector of military items, who not being a specialist in those fields would find the items too costly to include in a general collection of curios.

6: Restoration and display

The question of restoration is always a tricky one, as what is considered as legitimate restoration by one collector might be considered as faking or making up by another. There are, naturally, certain rules governing restoration but it is up to the individual to decide exactly how far and to what extent he wishes to go. Some collectors prefer to have an item in the condition they purchased it, even if parts are missing, and only to clean the piece; while others would consider it perfectly legitimate to add contemporary parts and to supply the item, if a head-dress, with plumes which very rarely survive the ravages of time. This addition of parts, and whether re-gilding is preferable to just cleaning the worn gilt that is there, is a personal decision. Below will be explained the various methods and ways of going about restoring or cleaning the items discussed in this book. To facilitate reference, they will be taken in the order they appear in the book.

(a) UNIFORMS

Whatever the apparent condition of any part of a uniform when purchased, a careful inspection should be undertaken of every inch of every seam to find if there is any trace of moth or grubs. If any are found, they should be carefully brushed out and a proprietary brand of spray used along and around the area. The outside of the uniform should be carefully brushed with not too stiff a brush to dislodge any dust in the fibre. Great care should be taken when brushing around lace on a jacket, tunic or coatee as any brisk hard strokes could snap the thread by which it is held or worse still catch in the weave of the lace and tear some of the threads. Items which are not too frail nor delicate and which need a good clean because they are stained can be dry cleaned. A word of warning, however, before this is undertaken, as this process if done by inexpert hands could irrevocably ruin a valuable piece. The item should be given *only* to a military tailor who is conversant with full dress uniforms. There are a number of reputable military tailors still in existence, especially in London, who would undertake this work which, because of its delicate nature and the fact that it will be done by hand, would not be inexpensive.

To clean the buttons on a jacket, tunic or coatee it is definitely not desirable to remove them and then to clean and re-sew. Try to obtain an army button stick which was designed for just this purpose or, failing that, take a large piece of stiff card or plastic and cut a slot to take the shank of the button when the card is slid under it. Brass buttons on other ranks' tunics can be cleaned with any good brass cleaner and then, if desired, lacquered to preserve their shine. Silver buttons can also be cleaned in this way with a good quality silver cleaner. Gilt buttons will have to be treated in a different manner. The act of rubbing with a polish or liquid will only serve to destroy the gilding on the button and will eventually reveal the brass. To undertake this job, place the button stick in position and surround the area with a number of crumpled tissues. Then taking a piece of cotton wool, dip it in a solution of ammonia and water and gently rub over the button. If the button is in reasonable condition with much of the gilt remaining a high shine will be obtained and much of the discoloration and dirt will be removed.

Except for other ranks' tunics, coatees and jackets, those of the officers in the main were decorated in some manner with gold or silver lace. Age has usually tarnished the lace and in some cases this appears almost black because of oxidisation. Here the best remedy is the professional one. Take the item to a military tailor conversant with this type of work or one of the firms which still supply gold lace. There are a number of these still in existence in London and some in the provinces. Once again, because of the delicate nature of the work and the fact that it will be done by hand, it will not be cheap.

Other ranks' tunics will usually come up well when expertly dry cleaned as the sewn-on items such as chevrons, regimental designation on the shoulder straps and any skill-at-arms badges will respond to the cleaning of the material of the item.

If the stains on the tunic are not too bad or the lace not tarnished then it can be cleaned by the collector himself. The method to use is that quoted in Dress Regulations and is reproduced here in full.

Care and Preservation of Uniform and of Gold Lace
(extracted from Dress Regulations 1934)

Before being packed away, gold lace, braid, cord or buttons on garments should be covered with tissue paper (*sulphur free*) and then placed in tin-lined air-tight cases . . . For the prevention of moths, the garment should be well aired and brushed before being packed.

Tarnished gold lace, braid, cord and embroidery can be cleaned by first well brushing, and then brushing with clean, dry pipe-clay. If this fails, a teaspoonful of cream of tartar and one pint of bread-crumbs (the latter should be one or two days old) should be rubbed up very finely and brushed lightly over the tarnished parts with a clean, soft brass brush.

Scarlet Clothing

(i) It is essential to remember that scarlet cloth, either as a garment or as a trimming, requires special treatment. SALTS OF SORREL or OXALIC ACID should never be used on scarlet clothing.

(ii) *Button or hook stains*—Rub dry pipe-clay over the stained part and brush with a clean hard brush.

(iii) *Oil and grease stains*—Rub the stain lightly with a small piece of scarlet or white cloth saturated with trichlorethylene spirit, or with a clean brush. If the stain is persistent it is much better to allow the spirit to run over and off the stained part than to rub it continually, as excessive rubbing tends to remove the dye, but it may be found necessary to apply similar treatment a second time. In all cases, even with persistent stains, light rubbing or brushing is advisable. It is important that the direction of the rubbing or brushing should always be towards the centre of the stain, as to rub outwards may spread the stain and also cause marks or rings to be formed round it. When first applying the spirit it is advisable to place underneath the stain a piece of white blotting-paper in order to absorb the liquid after it has penetrated the stained part.

For other ranks' clothing, 'Regulations for the Clothing of the Army —Part 1 Regular Forces 1926' recommends that: Garments and caps which have become soiled or dirty . . . can be cleaned with hot water and good quality yellow soap applied with a stiff nail brush. The soap should be placed in a clean bowl of hot water and allowed to dissolve. For stains caused by solids or liquids which have contained sugar, *e.g.* tea or coffee, a little methylated spirit should be rubbed lightly over the garment or stained parts with a clean brush.

In some cases the collector will come across tunics and coatees which have been stripped of their gold or silver lace. In some cases this has been preserved with the item but more often than not it has disappeared. The usual culprit of this stripping off of lace is a person ignorant of what the item is and even more ignorant in thinking that the gold or silver lace is of high value. This is not to say that scrap lace does not have any value: it certainly does, but only in some considerable quantity. If the lace is with the tunic then all it needs is to be replaced. Unless you are an expert in this matter it is best to confide the job to a professional military tailor who will know exactly how the lace should be applied and how the various curves and corners should be sewn. If the lace is missing this will present a problem to the collector. The author knew of at least one collector who used to snap up any tunics minus lace because they were sold cheaply, only to find that he was unable to replace the lace.

If you have acquired a tunic, jacket or coatee minus its lace the major problem will be to ascertain exactly what the original lace was like as there are many regimental patterns in Britain alone besides those in use in Europe and America. If the item is foreign then the obvious source of new lace will be the country of origin. Lace is still profusely made in France and many of the old patterns of Imperial German and Austrian lace are still made mainly for the film industries. If the lace you require is for a British item, then recourse should be made to one of the military lacemakers but here your quest might be fruitless. Regimental lace was produced in abundance in the era of full dress, various patterns in various widths for every part of the uniform and equipment, but decline in the demand and the minimum economical lengths a lacemaker will weave have reduced the pre-war stocks considerably. In some cases you might be lucky to get exactly the lace you require. This will probably be in the case of the Foot Guards and Household Cavalry whose lace is still made, and perhaps the infantry of the line after 1881 which had the rose pattern lace for English regiments, and thistle lace for Scottish and shamrock for Irish regiments. Rifle regiments' black mohair lace will also probably be available as will the lace and cording for the Royal Horse Artillery. The main problem will be in the various cavalry pattern laces, very little of which remains.

For the older items of pre-Crimean vintage, the finding of lace will be even more difficult as will be the discovering of the exact pattern used. Here guidance can probably be obtained from the regimental museum concerned, or by reference to lacemakers' and tailors' pattern books in some museum collections.

The remarks above on gold lace apply equally to those items of equipment such as cross-belts, pouches, sabretaches, shabraques and epaulettes. The cleaning and repair of these items should be handled only by a specialist in this work, who will know how to repair damaged and broken threads and restore as well as possible the tarnished lace and embroidery without ruining it.

The work of cleaning embroidered items and also their repair can be undertaken by, amongst others, the following concerns:

Messrs Hobson and Son, 154 Tooley Street, London S.E.1.
Messrs Hand, Lexington Street, London W.1.
Messrs Fabb Bros, Weldeck House, Weldeck Street, Maidenhead, Berks.

(This lacemaker will probably also be able to supply foreign designs of lace to order as they are specialists in film costume work.)

(b) HEAD-DRESS

The restoration and cleaning of head-dress is probably more difficult and requires more patience than any other cleaning work in this field. It is necessary to state that unless you feel fully confident that you are capable of undertaking the task you should not do it as a helmet or shako worth many pounds can be reduced to the value of a few pounds worth of spare parts when tackled by inexpert hands. Head-dress can be roughly divided into four types when it comes to cleaning or restoration work: cloth, such as tricorns, bicorns and mitre caps; metal, such as heavy cavalry helmets; leather, such as the *Pickelhaube* and Russian Crimean helmets, and felt or beaver, such as various pattern shakos. There are also the hussar busbies, the most difficult items to restore, and fur grenadier caps where little or nothing can be done to preserve them once in bad condition.

For hats such as tricorns and bicorns, careful brushing will usually restore some of the former lustre and remove dust and moths' eggs, but if in doubt the item can usually be cleaned, including any gold or silver lace tassels, by a military hatmaker or tailor. Embroidered mitre caps will present more of a problem as usually they will be in a fairly bad condition when acquired and need a great amount of expert work to clean and repair. Here, because of the amount of gold or silver embroidery, they should be tackled by a lacemaker, but careful instructions must be given detailing exactly the amount and extent of the work to be undertaken.

Metal helmets present less of a problem for the collector and can usually be cleaned quite well without taking the entire item to pieces. The badge will probably be held with nuts which should be carefully removed and put safely aside while the badge is cleaned. Most badges on metal head-dresses are made up of various component parts in either gilt or silver or a combination of the two. The parts are sometimes held with nuts but more often than not with metal pins. These should be carefully removed with a pair of long-nosed pliers, making sure that the surface of the plate is not scratched. When doing this work it is advisable to place the helmet plate or badge on a bed of thick felt or cotton wool. Once the various pieces have been cleaned they should be reassembled using the original pins.

Plumes on metal helmets are usually detachable and should be removed before work is undertaken on the skull. Here a gentle clean over with a good quality metal polish should suffice even though there are parts still on the skull difficult to clean around without leaving an unsightly film of dried polish. A very soft toothbrush should be useful for getting into these difficult corners. As the parts mentioned are usually riveted, their removal should only be attempted by an expert. Plumes can be cleaned usually by plunging them into warm water and soap suds suitable for woollens, etc. They should be gently cleaned by rubbing with a soft brush and then hung to dry *naturally*, after which they should be brushed and combed as one would do a wig.

Many heavy cavalry helmets employed a fur crest, usually of bearskin, but very few *originals* have survived to this day. If you are fortunate enough to acquire a helmet with its *original* crest great care should be taken with it as the slightest handling could bring tufts falling out and any attempt to brush it would be fatal. It is here that one of those problems for collectors will arise. Some will say that the old skin and fur should be stripped off as it will not only be unsightly but unhealthy, and new fur put on the old frame, whereas others would be for keeping the original, however unsightly. It is a choice for the collector himself. It would be very difficult, if not impossible, to restore the old fur let alone arrest the moulting and very few people would undertake work on fur so deteriorated. The same problem applies to busbies, which for officers were made from fur, although in this latter case small pieces of fur can be patched in or, if long enough, the fur brushed carefully over the offending hole.

Leather helmets are more of a problem than they seem to be at first. If in fair condition the various components, which will probably be held with small leather strips passed through the shanks of the parts, should be removed. It is usually fairly difficult to save these pieces of leather and when reassembling facsimile pieces should be cut and fitted. The skull, usually still with its rim riveted to the peak, should be carefully cleaned with good quality boot polish before the other cleaned parts are remounted. The leather on a skull in inferior condition will be soft, shapeless, or mis-shapen and flaking. A product such as neetsfoot oil or heel ball should be carefully applied to try to re-vitalise the leather. If it is misshapen then some sort of block must be made to restore the original shape. An expanding wig block is sometimes suitable or ideally a hatmaker's block. Any discrepancy in size of shape can be made up by using tissue paper. When the skull seems to have taken up its original form, it can then be lightly polished before the parts are reassembled. It is prudent when displaying an item restored in this way to block out the inside with tissue paper, as otherwise it might over a period of time start to return to its shapelessness.

(Blue cloth helmets are similar to *Pickelhaubes* in shape and should be stripped down in the same manner. The cloth can then be brushed firmly with a stiff clothes brush.)

Leather helmets, such as tarletons, are best given to experts to clean and restore as the metal parts are usually riveted to the leather. The crest of fur will also present the same problem as the heavy cavalry helmets mentioned above.

Shakos made of felt or beaver, and in some cases of lacquered leather, should be carefully stripped of their component parts which will usually be found to be held with small leather thongs. The metal parts can then be cleaned: gilt with ammonia, silver and brass with polish or, if desired, they can be re-gilded. This applies to all restoration mentioned above. The body of the shako will commonly be found to be of cloth and the peak, top and head band in leather. Originally this was patent leather but in nearly every case it will be found to be melted and bubbled through bad and long storage. Nothing can be done with this except for a gentle clean with good boot polish but where the condition is not too bad the old army boot trick of a warm spoon and melted polish could be tried but it is risky and could completely ruin an otherwise valuable piece. The felt part should be carefully brushed but make sure that the bristles are soft, as a hard bristle could catch and tear the thin material.

Great care should be taken with the linings of head-dresses. As a rule the original lining, however bad, should be retained as this often bears the maker's trade label and enhances the value of the piece.

In many cases damage to helmets will be in the form of the chin chain or scales coming unsewn from their backing. At first sight this appears to be an easy task but it is not just a matter of sewing the chains or scales back to the leather. The leather part will be found to be in two halves joined along the edge by stitching. This will have to be undone, the two parts separated, the chain or scales sewn to one half and then the other part stitched on to hide the cross stitching. Missing chin chains can be replaced if one is lucky enough to have a spares box or to be able to acquire one and fortunately these are fairly easy to come by. Tapered chin chains such as those used on Guards' bearskins, are still made as they originally were but parallel ones, used on dragoon and blue cloth helmets which are still made today are of thinner brass and the rings are slightly smaller. Other missing items such as spikes, cavalry helmet plume holders, rosettes to hold the chin chain can still, with luck, be found. Reproductions of rosettes and lion heads for lancer caps are still made but these too tend to be thinner and the lion heads are minus the screw and hook fitments.

Helmet restoration is a difficult and exacting task and unless you feel fully capable of tackling it, don't! One specialist in helmet repair and restoration who undertakes even the most delicate work and produces high quality work is: A. A. Fordham, 89 Tile Kiln Lane, Hemel Hempstead, Herts. He will also be able to supply almost any sort of plume, in horsehair and feather and also worsted pompons for shakos in all sizes.

Colours, for those lucky enough to acquire them, should without hesitation be given to an experienced firm for repair. The majority of colours made for the army today are manufactured by Messrs Hobson and Sons, 154 Tooley Street, London S.E.1 who will undertake repair work, but precise instructions must be given. They will also repair such items as shabraques, pipe banners and trumpet banners.

Drums also are a specialised craft and unless one is expert at re-roping and fitting new skins it is better to have this work carried out professionally. Some of the emblazoned drums acquired might also need repair to the paintwork and expert restoration is undertaken by Potter & Co. of Aldershot who will also undertake the repair of maces and military musical instruments.

For work such as gilding or enamelling many local firms can be found but it is advisable to show them the piece, explain to them exactly the work required and inquire whether they are capable of undertaking it.

The question of display is a personal matter depending on taste, space available and of course the items to be shown. Whatever the method chosen, it must be capable of keeping the uniform, head-dress or whatever, free from dust, moths and air pollution. All of these over a period of time will gradually ruin a fine item and considerably reduce its value. Fortunately, except in the case of steel helmets or breastplates, rust is not an enemy much encountered in the collecting of military antiques of the nature described in this book.

If space is available, then usually the best answer is a glass case. These can often be picked up fairly cheaply and easily as large department stores and shops modernise and alter their premises with remarkable frequency these days. However, a glass case of reasonable appearance can be constructed with not too much difficulty and there are many pre-fabricated units of shelving on the market today which only need the addition of a glass front to transform them into a display case. If the room in which you wish to display your collection, or part of it, has an alcove then you have an almost ready-made display corner.

If you are unable to keep your collection out, a good idea is to convert a wardrobe to house the various items. Once the basic wardrobe has been purchased then all that is required is a conversion of the interior. Strip out the existing shelves etc, and then line the inside with a material to form the background. The felt-like material with peel-off adhesive backs are good for this sort of work. Once this has been done, it is only necessary to plan the interior taking into account how many shelves you require for head-dresses and curios, and how much hanging space for tunics, coatees, drum major's sashes, etc. Once you have placed your collection you can then open it up for view or shut it away from dust and light as you wish.

If, on the other hand, you are unable to display any part, then the various items should be well protected before being stored away. Any cloth items and head-dress are best well cleaned and then wrapped in large plastic bags. Uniforms etc, can with the aid of a cloth hanger be stored in a wardrobe along with other clothes and head-dress, and other items can be put in drawers or cupboards without any risk of injury. One important point to remember about display is that sunlight will in time fade colours and the position of windows should be taken into account when planning your display. Artificial light, to some extent, also damages fabric so not too strong a light should be used to highlight or spotlight a rare or important item.

The new National Army Museum housed at Chelsea has defeated this menace by having lit showcases containing the items, but in a darkened room. Not only is the collection well protected but it also forms a pleasing light in which to view and study.

Items with gold or silver lace and embroidery are best protected by storing in thoroughly dry sulphur-free tissue paper before being wrapped in plastic bags. On *no account* bundle items such as belts, slings, etc, of gold or silver lace together with rubber or elastic bands as the action of the band with the air and gold lace will produce a black line which is impossible to remove.

The Black and White Plates

1. British: Officer's mitre cap, 43rd Foot (Grenadier Company) 1740–49

2. British: Grenadier's fur cap 1768 pattern

3. British: Infantry shako 1812–16

4. British: Officer's lance cap, 9th Lancers *circa* 1816

5. British: Left to right: officer's helmet, Leicestershire Yeomanry *circa* 1855; jug showing patriotic scene of 42nd Highland piper 'playing on a new instrument'; officer's helmet East Lothian Yeomanry, 'Albert' pattern *circa* 1860

6. British: Troop-Sergeant-Major's lance cap, 17th Lancers *circa* 1850
7. British: Officer's helmet, 6th Dragoon Guards 1847–66

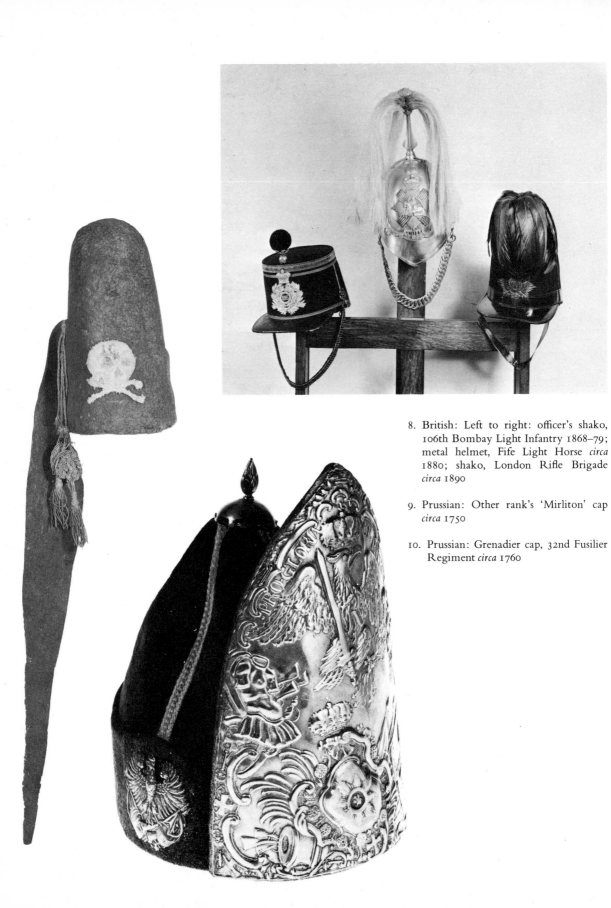

8. British: Left to right: officer's shako, 106th Bombay Light Infantry 1868–79; metal helmet, Fife Light Horse *circa* 1880; shako, London Rifle Brigade *circa* 1890

9. Prussian: Other rank's 'Mirliton' cap *circa* 1750

10. Prussian: Grenadier cap, 32nd Fusilier Regiment *circa* 1760

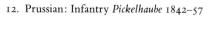
12. Prussian: Infantry *Pickelhaube* 1842–57

11. Prussian: Infantry pattern shako 1813–17

13. Prussian: *Feldmutze* 10th *Landwehr* Hussar Regiment
1843–52

14. Prussian: Lance cap or *czapka*, 3rd Lancer Regiment 1844–62

15. German: Left to right: *Pickelhaube*, 33rd or 34th Infantry *circa* 1900; felt lance cap, Guard *Uhlan* Regiment or 13th *Uhlan* Regiment *circa* 1914; *Pickelhaube*, Wurttemburg *Landwehr circa* 1900

16. German: *Garde du Corps* helmet *circa* 1900

17. Bavarian: Infantry *casquet circa* 1790

18. French: Lance cap, 1st Empire

19. French: Infantry shako with plate marked 'N 1ᴿ' '54', 1st Empire

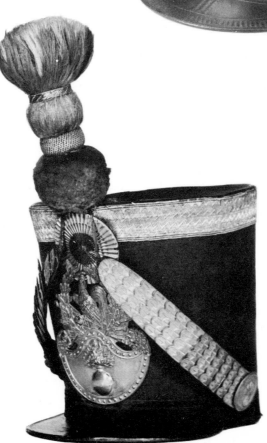

20. French: Infantry shako *circa* 1833

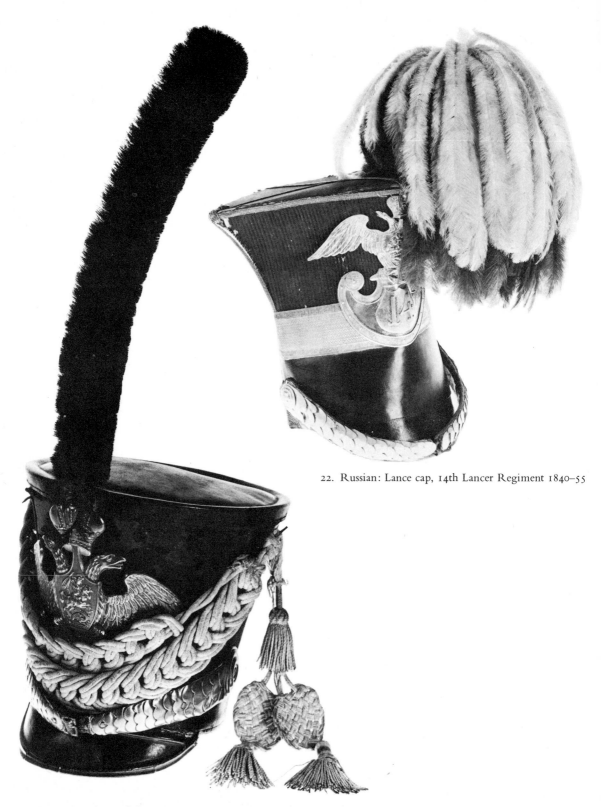

22. Russian: Lance cap, 14th Lancer Regiment 1840–55

21. Russian: Infantry shako 1840–46

23. Russian: Left: helmet of Guard Infantry. Right: helmet of General Officer.
1844–60

24. Russian: Officer's *kepi* 1862–81

25. Russian: Kiver of General of Cavalry 1908–14

26. American: Painted, leather-fronted mitre cap, New-
port Light Infantry *circa* 1778

27. American: Tricorn hat 1775

28. American: Light Dragoon-style helmet *circa* 1814

29. American: 1872 pattern cavalry helmet

30. American: 1872 pattern infantry *kepi*

31. American: 1881 pattern infantry spiked helmet

32. British: Infantry private 1742

33. British: Other rank's coat, 1st Regiment Foot Guards
circa 1772

COLDSTREAM GUARDS
PRIVATE, GRENADIER COMPANY, 1792.

34. British: Private, Grenadier Company Coldstream Guards 1792

35. British: Officers of 12th Light Dragoons. The plate shows the 'Tarleton' style helmet and the regimental guidon in the background. 1794

36. British: Corporal, Grenadier Company 3rd Foot Guards 1815

37. British: Lieutenant-General The Hon. Henry Beauchamp Lygon, Colonel 10th Hussars 1843

38. British: Officer, 5th Dragoon Guards *circa* 1848

39. British: Private, 28th Foot in full marching Order, Crimea 1855

Facing page:

40. British: Officers and men, 93rd Highlanders, Crimea 1855

41. British: Officer, 12th Foot *circa* 1860

42. British: The Prince of Wales in the uniform of the Rifle Brigade *circa* 1866

43. British: N.C.O.s and men of the Household Cavalry, left to right: Trumpeter, 1st Life Guards; Private, 1st Life Guards; Corporal, 1st Life Guards; Corporal-Major, Royal Horse Guards. 1861

44. British: Officers, colour sergeants and colours of 24th Foot 1880

45. British: Private, South Wales Borderers 1910

Dress Sword Knot half size.

Undress Waist Belt Lace, full size.

Back of Dress Jacket.

Half front of Dress Jacket.

Cuff.

Front View of Chacko

Side View of Chacko

N.B. Lace for Trowsers Jacket and Shabraque - Vandyke Pattern.

Adjutant General's Office,
Fort Saint George,
1st September 1846.

46. British: East India Company's Army. Lithographed plate showing jacket and shako of Madras Light Cavalry 1846

47. British: Indian Army. Officers of 35th Scinde Horse 1911

49. French: Private Royal Regiment mid-18th century

48. French: Infantry private, 99th Regiment 1715–49

50. French: Hussar *circa* 1770

51. French: Drummer and line infantryman, 1st
Empire

53. French: Light Infantrymen *circa* 1846

54. French: *Cuirassiers*: left to right: 1680, 1750, 1789–94, 1809, 1830, 1840

55. French: Dragoons: left to right: 1700, 1750, 1789, 1810, 1824, 1840

56. French: Hussars: left to right: 1680, 1760, 1794, 1810, 1824, 1840

57. French: *Chasseurs d'Afrique* in the Crimea 1855. Note the loose trousers and the *casquette d'Afrique*

58. French: Chasseur *circa* 1870

59. French: Horse Artillery *circa* 1870

60. French: Various uniforms of the infantry 1600s to 1908

61. Prussian: Officer, *Garde du Corps circa* 1790

62. Prussian: Officer, *Garde du Corps* 1809

63. Prussian: Officer of *Garde Fusilier Bataillon* 1809

Grenadier des Normal Infanterie Bataillons

64. Prussian: Grenadier private of infantry 1809

65. Prussian: Officers and men of the *Garde du Corps* in Gala dress with *surveste*

Garde du Corps.

66. German: German Kaiser in tropical uniform *circa* 1896

67. Russian: Troopers of the Regiment of Horse Guards *circa* 1835

68. Russian: Officers in (left to right) walking out dress, full dress winter, full dress summer. Guard Grenadier Regiment Pavlowsky *circa* 1835

Facing page:

69. Russian: Grenadiers in winter dress and sergeant in summer dress. Guard Grenadier Regiment Pavlowsky *circa* 1835

70. Swedish: Infantryman, Södermanland Regiment pattern 1756
71. Swedish: Trooper, Cuirassier Corps of the Life Guards 1795
72. Swedish: Infantry uniforms 1820–30s. Left to right: 2nd Life Guards, Smaland
    Grenadier Battalion, Svea Life Guards, Grenadier Corps of Lige Regiment, 1st
    Life Grenadier Regiment

73. Swedish: Cavalry uniforms 1820–30s. Left to right: Jamland Mounted Squadron,
    Dragoon Corps of Life Regiment, Horse Guards, Scanian Dragoon Regiment,
    Crown Prince's Hussar Regiment
74. Swedish: Trooper Horse Guards 1845 wearing Prussian-style helmet
75. Swedish: Vastgota Regiment infantryman pattern 1860
76. Swedish: Life Regiment Hussar Corps 1870

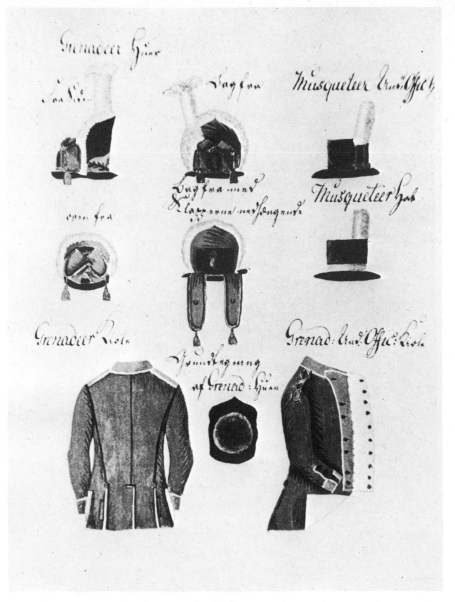

77. Danish: Contemporary drawings of grenadier cap and coat 1789

78. Danish: Officer of the Royal Horse Guard *circa* 1804
79. Danish: Musketeers of 2nd Jutland Regiment 1828
80. Danish: Infantryman 1842

81. Danish: Dragoons 1858
82. Danish: The *Gardehussarregiment* on winter manœuvres wearing the pelisse 1886

83. Danish: Infantryman 1910

84. Austro–Hungarian: Line infantry 1800
85. Austro–Hungarian: Line infantry 1830

86. Austro–Hungarian: Hussars 1850

87. Austro–Hungarian: Line infantry 1900

88. Austro–Hungarian: Dragoons 1914. Left to right: sergeant-major, corporal, trooper

89. American: Officer's coat,
New York Militia *circa* 1777

90. American: Brigadier-General's uniform *circa* 1809 with
lapels buttoned back and coat
hooked

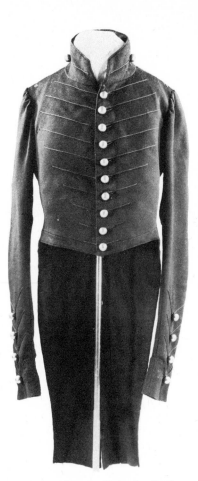

91. American: General Staff
Officer's coatee 1821–31

92. American: Dragoon Sergeant, winter dress 1833–50

93. American: Dress uniforms, Union infantryman *circa* 1864

94. American: Fatigue uniform, Civil War period 1865

95. American: Sergeant, Light Artillery 1864–71
96. American: Infantryman, 5th New York Volunteers Infantry (Zouaves). One of the number of regiments on both sides during the Civil War which adopted Zouave-style uniforms

97. American: Captain's coat, Confederate State Artillery *circa* 1865

98. British: Household Cavalry breastplate and back-plate, *circa* 1820
99. Belgian: Cuirassiers' helmet and breastplate and back-plate *circa* 1850

100. French: Cuirassiers' helmet and breastplate and back-plates *circa* 1845
101. Russian: Officer's helmet and cuirass, Life Guard Horse Guard *circa* 1860

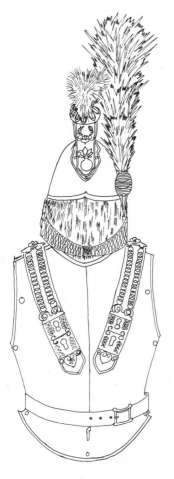

102. British: Sabretache, 16th Light Dragoons *circa* 1799
103. British: Sabretache, 5th Dragoon Guards *circa* 1815

104. British: Sabretache, 11th Hussars *circa* 1865
105. British: Undress pouch and sabretache. Westmorland and Cumberland Yeomanry *circa* 1880

106. French: Sabretache, Republican 9th Regiment of Cavalry *circa* 1790
107. Russian: Sabretache, Life Guard Hussar Regiment 1855–81

108. British: Epaulette, Commissariat Staff Corps officer *circa* 1816
109. Austrian/Bavarian: Austrian pouch, Austrian pouch, Bavarian pouch and belt

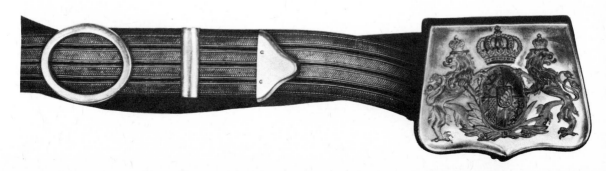

110. British: Rear view of a hussar trooper's equipment *circa* 1855 (reproduction)
111. British: Infantry pattern equipment *circa* 1850 consisting of knapsack, mess tin in oilskin cover, cross-belt for bayonet, cross-belt for pouch and water canteen

112. American: Infantry equipment *circa* 1850 consisting of waistbelt with clasp, small pouch for percussion caps, cross-belt and large pouch

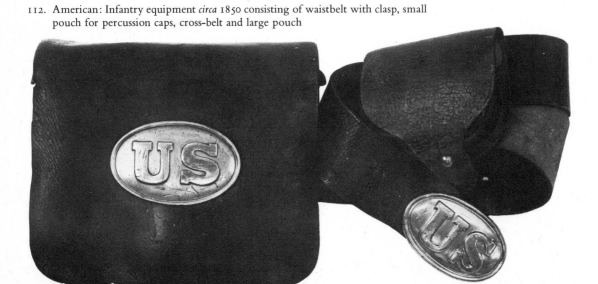

113. British: Officer's shabraque, 3rd Dragoon Guards 1847

114. German: Various patterns of shabraques and horse furniture *circa* 1890

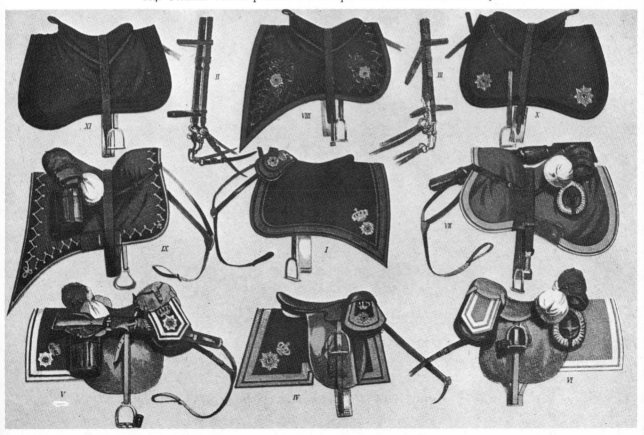

115. British: Selection of cavalry-sergeant's arm badges, regular and yeomanry

116. British: Cross-belt plates. Top row left to right: 83rd Foot 1840–50, Coldstream Guards *circa* 1831, Royal Artillery 1833–48. Centre row left to right: 31st Foot (*Note:* numbers on plate have been reversed after cleaning in error), 49th Foot 1843–55, 74th Foot *circa* 1875. Bottom row left to right: Royal Marine Light Infantry *circa* 1850, 28th Foot *circa* 1850, 7th Foot Light Company *circa* 1812

117. British: Helmet plate, collar badge and waistbelt clasp, 1st Berwick Rifle Volunteer Corps *circa* 1880. From original pattern drawing

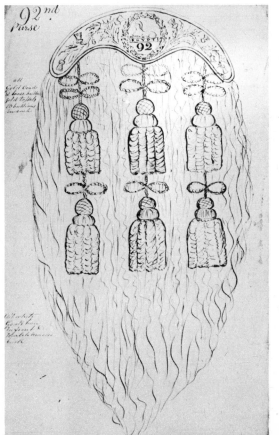

118. British: Gorgets, shako plates and beltplates: Gorget, Dunfirmilin Volunteers *circa* 1810; shako plate, East Middlesex Militia *circa* 1850; Gorget *circa* 1800; waistbelt clasp, heavy cavalry *circa* 1815; cross-belt plate, Honourable East India Company *circa* 1800; cross-belt plate, King's Own Borderers *circa* 1860; helmet plate, 1st Volunteer Battalion Middlesex Regiment *circa* 1905; cross-belt plate, 57th Foot *circa* 1850

119. British: Pattern book drawing of 92nd purse or sporran *circa* 1848

For the Defence of Old England.

THE KING having been pleased to shew his Approbation of The ROYAL LANCASHIRE VOLUNTEERS, by expressing his Desire that the Regiment might be kept as compleat as possible; Sir THOMAS EGERTON, Baronet, Lieutenant-Colonel Commandant, *Takes this METHOD of acquainting*

All Lancashire LADS of SPIRIT,

That there are a few Vacancies in that Corps which must be immediately filled up.

Any Young Men of five Feet seven Inches, or upwards, who are ambitious to become GENTLEMEN VOLUNTEERS, and to have their Names enrolled in the List of those who **have boldly** stood forth the Champions of their Country, have now an **Opportunity** of shewing their Zeal and Affection for the best of Kings, **and their** Detestation of the Perfidy of the Enemies of OLD ENGLAND. Those who are desirous of this Honour, may apply to Lieutenant-Colonel Commandant,

Sir THOMAS EGERTON, Bart. at Heaton House.

Or to Serjeant-Major

Sir ASHTON LEVER, Knight, at Alkrington,
OR AT

The Head-Quarters, the Bull's-Head Inn, in this Town.

These Gentlemen propose with a Martial Band of Music and Colours flying, to beat up for VOLUNTEERS at *Manchester*, on *Saturday* next, at Eleven o'Clock in the Forenoon, at which Time and Place they hope to have the Honour of the Attendance of all Lovers of their *King* and *Country*, and Friends to The ROYAL LANCASHIRE VOLUNTEERS.

The Vacancies are so few, and the Time so short, wherein they will be filled up, that those who wish not to lose this Occasion of handing down their Names with Glory to Posterity along with their Friends and Neighbours, in a Regiment, which on Account of it's steady Behaviour, had the Honour of being the sole Guard at his Majesty's ROYAL PALACES, at *Windsor, Hampton Court, Richmond,* and *Kew,* during the late Disturbances in *London,* must apply immediately.

They will have every Degree of Attention paid to them whilst in the Regiment: They cannot be sent out of *Great-Britain,* nor drafted into any other Corps; but at the end of their Service, they will be disbanded in their own County, and return crowned with Laurels to the peaceable Enjoyment of their Property, for the Defence of which they have so nobly stood forth.

G O D Save the K I N G.

Manchester, Sept. 27, 1780.

120. British: Recruiting poster for Royal Lancashire Volunteers

121. Post cards including British, French and German. Note the various illustrated ones and the First World War prisoner and troop correspondence cards

122. Curios: 'Gentleman in khaki' 1900; ashtray in the form of a peaked cap made from an 18 pdr shell case; German prisoner-of-war medallion made in the Isle of Man; 'Gentleman in khaki' medallion 1900

123. Curios: Princess Mary's Gift Fund cigarette box and bullet pencil, Christmas 1914

125. Swedish: Side drum *circa* 1700

126. British: Side drum, 42nd Highlanders *circa* 1820

124. British: Drum-Major's sash, 5th Northumberland Fusiliers

127. British: Coldstream Guards colour *circa* 1820

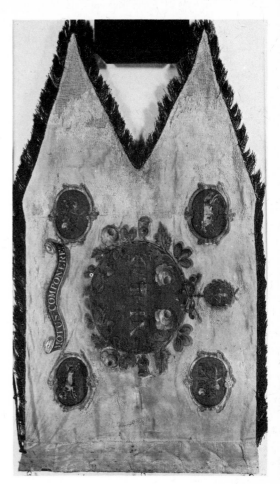

128. British: 11th Light Dragoon's guidon *circa* 1780

129. Russian: Regimental colour, Seminov Life Guard Regiment 1700   130. Swedish: Artillery colour 1716

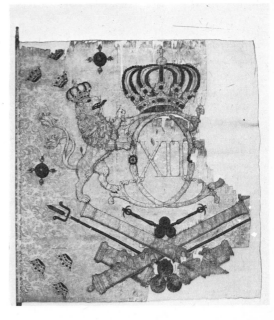

Illustration Credits

Colour

Wilkinson–Latham collection except plates 7, 8, 9, 10 which are produced by permission of the Musée de L'Armée, Paris.

Black and white

Heeresgeschtliches Museum, Vienna: 84, 85, 86, 87, 88

Kungl. Armemuseum, Stockholm: 9, 70, 71, 72, 73, 74, 75, 76, 125, 129, 130

Musée de L'Armée, Paris: 54, 55, 56

Musée Royal de L'Armée and D'Histoire Militaire, Brussels: 10, 11, 12, 13, 14, 21, 22, 106

Mollo Collection: 7, 23, 25, 101, 107, 110

National Army Museum, London: 1, 33, 39, 45, 57, 126

Parker Gallery, London: 4, 6, 8, 26, 32, 34, 35, 37, 42, 59, 98, 102, 104, 108, 113, 116, 120, 128

T. O. Read Collection: 2, 3, 5

Scottish United Services Museum, Edinburgh: 36

Smithsonian Institution, Washington: 27, 28, 29, 30, 31, 89, 90, 91, 92, 93, 94, 95, 96, 97

Tøjhusmuseet, Copenhagen: 77, 78, 79, 80, 81, 82, 83

Wallis and Wallis (R. Butler Esq.) Lewes: 15, 16, 17, 18, 19, 20, 99, 105, 109, 111, 112, 115, 127

Wilkinson–Latham Collection: 38, 40, 41, 43, 44, 46, 47, 48, 49, 50, 51, 52, 53, 58, 60, 61, 62, 63, 64, 65, 66, 67, 68, 69, 100, 114, 117, 118, 119, 121, 122, 123, 124

Appendix 1 : Museums

All European and many American countries have museums, either local or national, which deal to some extent with their armed forces. These institutions will be found to be most helpful with serious inquiries and nearly all have a photographic service which, for a sum, would supply black and white photographs of various items. Many, too, publish illustrated guide books and some of those in Scandinavian museums are written in English. Some museums, because of the vastness of their collections, do not publish an illustrated catalogue but keep a huge index system so that any item can be found. Probably not all their material is on show because of lack of space but most museums will allow the serious student to inspect items off display if ample warning is given. The museums besides having display areas will usually have a library or archives section where, with prior warning, books and documents may be examined.

It is worthwhile, however, before an expected visit, to obtain the necessary permission or pass well in advance as this will save time and headache later on. Besides the national museums listed below there are many other local or regimental foreign museums which have displays of military interest. *Soldier* Magazine, Clayton Barracks, Aldershot, Hants. GU11 2BG have published a useful list of military museums and at the moment (1973) are running a series on museums of military interest.

Great Britain: National Army Museum, Royal Hospital Road, London SW3 4HT
Scottish United Service Museum, Crown Square, The Castle, Edinburgh
Austria: Heeresgeschichtliches Museum, 1030 Wien, Arsenal, Obj 1
Belgium: Musee Royal de L'Armee et Histoire Militaire, Parc du Cinquantenaire 3, Brussels B 1040
Denmark: Tøjhusmuseet, 1220 København K, Frederiksholms Kanal 29
France: Musée de L'Armée, Paris
Germany (East): Museum für Deutsche Geschichte, Berlin
Italy: Museo Nazionale di Castel St. Angelo, Rome
Norway: Haermuseet, Akerhus, Oslo mil, Oslo 1
Poland: Polish Army Museum, Warsaw

Russia: State Historical Museum, Moscow
Spain: Museo del Ejercito, Calle Mendez Nunez, 1, Madrid 14
Sweden: Kungle Armemuseum, 103 82, Stockholm 7
United States of America: Smithsonian Institution, Washington D.C. 20560

Although there are other museums in these countries, those listed have the main military collections. Information concerning other museums in their country will usually be given when writing to any of the above as long as you list your particular interest.

Appendix 2: Where to buy

The question that invariably crops up in any field of collecting is—where to buy? There are three main courses open to the collector when he wishes to augment his collection and these are: auction sales, dealers and private advertising. To those who belong to a society such as the Military Historical Society there is always the chance at their monthly meetings of acquiring items from a fellow member via advertisements in their journal.

There are two auction houses that specialise entirely for the military collector and these are Wallis and Wallis of 210 High Street, Lewes, Sussex and Weller and Dufty Ltd., 141 Bromsgrove Street, Birmingham 5. Both hold monthly auction sales. Wallis and Wallis have anything up to about 2,000 lots while Weller and Dufty sell about 1,000 to 1,500. Both issue illustrated catalogues containing a price list of what the items in their previous sale realised, which will be a useful guide to values for the collector. The catalogues are carefully prepared and usually have lengthy descriptions and a section of black and white photographic illustrations of the more choice lots. This then, is the first avenue open to the collector but it must be emphasised that personal viewing and handling prior to the sale is indispensable. If unable to attend, seek the advice and opinion of a friend or dealer who is attending. Both houses state in their sale conditions that although every effort has been made to ensure accuracy, no warranty is given, nor are the auctioneers responsible for the authenticity of any items. So the best answer when buying 'under the hammer' is to inspect personally the item you are interested in; make your own decision as to its authenticity and value to *you*. A private buyer at an auction will find himself up against dealers as well as other private collectors so a word of caution to the novice: make up your mind beforehand exactly what your maximum price will be on a certain lot and stick to it. Usually dealers will not be able to place such a high price on an item as a private collector as they have to consider profit margins, overheads and other costs; even so, they are professionals and business men and usually know what they are doing when they bid large sums for something you consider worth only a few pounds.

The novice should tread warily at auction sales and should try to attend, even if he doesn't buy, to see the inner workings. The golden rule is to settle the value you place on the item prior to the sale as, on occasions, novice collectors will reach their limit and then go on in the vain hope that the next bid will secure it. This rarely works and usually the collector ends up paying far more than he intended. The other important rule is *not* to buy 'on spec' in an auction. It is easily done and rarely is a bargain obtained in this way. Whilst sitting waiting for a lot you are interested in, you see an item being held up that you recognise. The bidding starts and then stops at what you consider a ridiculous price. You bid, and secure it—only to find that it is either defective, has parts missing or modern replacement parts. You have learned; but it has probably been an expensive mistake that could easily have been avoided.

On occasion you will find that the item you are interested in also interests a number of dealers. Here there are two courses open to you. Either you try to outbid the dealers or you let the dealers bid amongst themselves and then, if the price is still not outside your scope, make a note of the purchaser. After the sale you can usually buy the item from the dealer at the price he paid plus a small profit for him, unless of course he has been instructed to buy by one of his clients.

If you are uncertain of either what price an item might fetch or its authenticity and need advice, a member of the auctioneer's staff should be consulted. Being themselves experts in this field, they are only to happy to aid and guide the novice collector. Studying price lists of previous sales is a good indication of prices of certain items but *must not* be taken as an absolute guide to their values, as the law of supply and demand applies here. If, say, a shako plate of the 33rd for the Waterloo shako sold for £65, then it doesn't means that one from the 57th would obtain the same price, because the purchaser of the 33rd plate might have been willing to pay well over the market value to fill a gap in his collection, or to obtain that one piece because he specialises in that unit. 185

The second main source of worthwhile items is dealers. As they scour the country and often travel abroad they have a better chance of acquiring a more varied selection of items. There are many specialised dealers in military antiques throughout the United Kingdom as well as in Europe and the United States, many offering rare as well as common items for sale in most price ranges. Dealers are usually willing to be on the look-out for you if you instruct them in exactly what you are looking for and your price range. Non-specialised and general dealers are well worth visiting as on occasion they turn up military items from sales of the contents of old houses, and it is worthwhile visiting such dealers and letting them know of your interests. Junk shops are also a source but these seem to be getting fewer and fewer these days. The main advantage of buying from an established dealer is that usually he is willing to vouch for an object's authenticity and give an indication of its age.

There is also a ready source of military items in street markets but here the buyer must make up his own mind about authenticity and value and buy accordingly as there is little chance of guaranteed authenticity from stallholders.

Advertising in specialist local or even national papers' personal columns can on occasion bring forth some interesting and rare items which have lain for years in a trunk or attic. There is, however, a caution to this form of buying. In some cases a person replying to your advertisement will state a price but more often than not they expect an offer from you. To honest collectors, the golden rule is to offer a fair price for the article, depending on its condition etc. In many cases items could be purchased at a fraction of what you give but if at any time the seller happens to tell of the transaction to someone who might be better acquainted with the value you will be branded as dishonest; whereas if you give a fair price the seller might recommend you to someone else who wishes to dispose of an item that might interest you and, because of your reputation of honesty, you will probably get first offer.

Selling and buying within a society of people of similar interests is also worthwhile as collectors frequently pick up items in a bulk lot that do not interest them and are willing to dispose of them, often at only a small profit. Also because it is a society of collectors with a common interest you will find that more often than not when your interests are known a fellow member will say that he has seen something in so and so's shop that might interest you. So you have a ready-made network looking out for items that appeal to you.

However, it cannot be too strongly emphasised that knowledge is all important in your hobby, or chosen sphere of your hobby. As with buying 'on spec' it is often dangerous to buy something you know nothing about because you think it is cheap. For what it is, it may well be very expensive. Books, visits to museums and discussions with other collectors are invaluable ways of increasing your knowledge. It is often wise to carry a notebook and make sketches and notes on items seen for future reference. Learning to recognise the shapes of items, the feel, and whether the metal is the right age or the leather of sufficient softness through wear are all important parts of the hobby. Here your notebook will come in handy. If you see something you are not sure about and might have made a note of, it will be invaluable; or if you see something you don't immediately recognise, don't trust to memory but draw it and note the relevant details until you can get to your books or discuss it with a fellow collector. Museums are always willing to give advice on what an object might be, but don't expect them to give a valuation or idea of price.

Many of the illustrations in this book come from museums and private collections but others have been selected from auction catalogues to show that fine items are still available. Many will argue against using photographs of rare items from museums, saying that they will never be available to collectors, but this is not so. Rare and old items still turn up and by learning to recognise the early designs and shapes you might find so-called 'unobtainable' pieces at probably not too high a price. A friend of the author once bought from a gun dealer a tarleton helmet (minus the fur crest) which the dealer had taken with a lot of weapons in a purchase made at a country sale. The price paid was 2s. 6d. for what was described as a leather jockey cap. The purchaser happened to recognise the shape as the helmet lay in a cardboard box of odds and ends when visiting the dealer's shop.

In pursuing your collecting, no avenue, however hopeless, should be left unexplored as it is amazing what is hidden in trunks and attics waiting to be found.

Bibliography

A History of the Uniforms of the British Army. C. C. P. Lawson, London 1940–67

Battle Dress. F. Wilkinson, London 1970

British Military Badges and Buttons. R. J. Wilkinson-Latham, Aylesbury 1973

British Military Uniforms from Contemporary Prints. W. Y. Carman, London 1957

Cavalry Uniforms of Britain and the Commonwealth. R. and C. Wilkinson-Latham, London 1969

Dix Siecles de Costumes Militaire. H. Lacouque, Paris 1965

Dress Regulations for the Army. London (various dates) 1822–1934

European Military Uniforms. P. Martin, London 1967

French Regiments and Uniforms. W. A. Thorburn, London 1969

German Weapons, Uniforms, Insignia 1841–1918. Major J. Hicks, U.S.A. 1963

Handbuch der Uniformkunde. Knotel and Sieg, Hamburg 1937

Handbook of the Russian Army in Asia. Major J. Woolfe-Murray, R.A., London 1890

Head Dress of the British Army–Cavalry. W. Y. Carman, Sutton 1968

Helmets and Head Dress of the Imperial German Army, 1870–1918. Colonel R. H. Rankin, U.S.A. 1965

Home Service Helmet, 1878–1914. R. and C. Wilkinson-Latham, London 1970

Infantry Uniforms of Britain and the Commonwealth. R. and C. Wilkinson-Latham, London 1970 and 1971

Military Drawings and Paintings in the Royal Collection. A. Hasewell-Miller and N. P. Dawney, London 1966 and 1970

Military Fashion. John Mollo, London 1972

Military Uniforms in Colour. P. Kannik, London 1968

New Regulations for the Prussian Infantry. London 1757

Rules and Regulations for the Sword Exercises of the Cavalry. London 1796

Sabretaches of the British Army. W. Y. Carman, London 1969

Schuler, Hartley and Graham Catalogue. U.S.A. reprint 1961

The Book of the Continental Soldier. Harold L. Peterson, U.S.A. 1968

The Development of the Mills Woven Cartridge Belt. A. A. Lethern, London 1965

Uniforms and Equipment of the Light Brigade. John and Boris Mollo, London 1968

United States Army Headgear to 1845. E. Howell and D. Kloster, U.S.A. 1969

Museum Catalogues

Tøjhusmuseet, Copenhagen
Kungl. Armemuseum, Stockholm

Journals

Journal of the Society of Army Historical Research
Bulletin of the Military Historical Society
Journal of the Royal United Services Institution
Tradition, London
Historama, France

Index